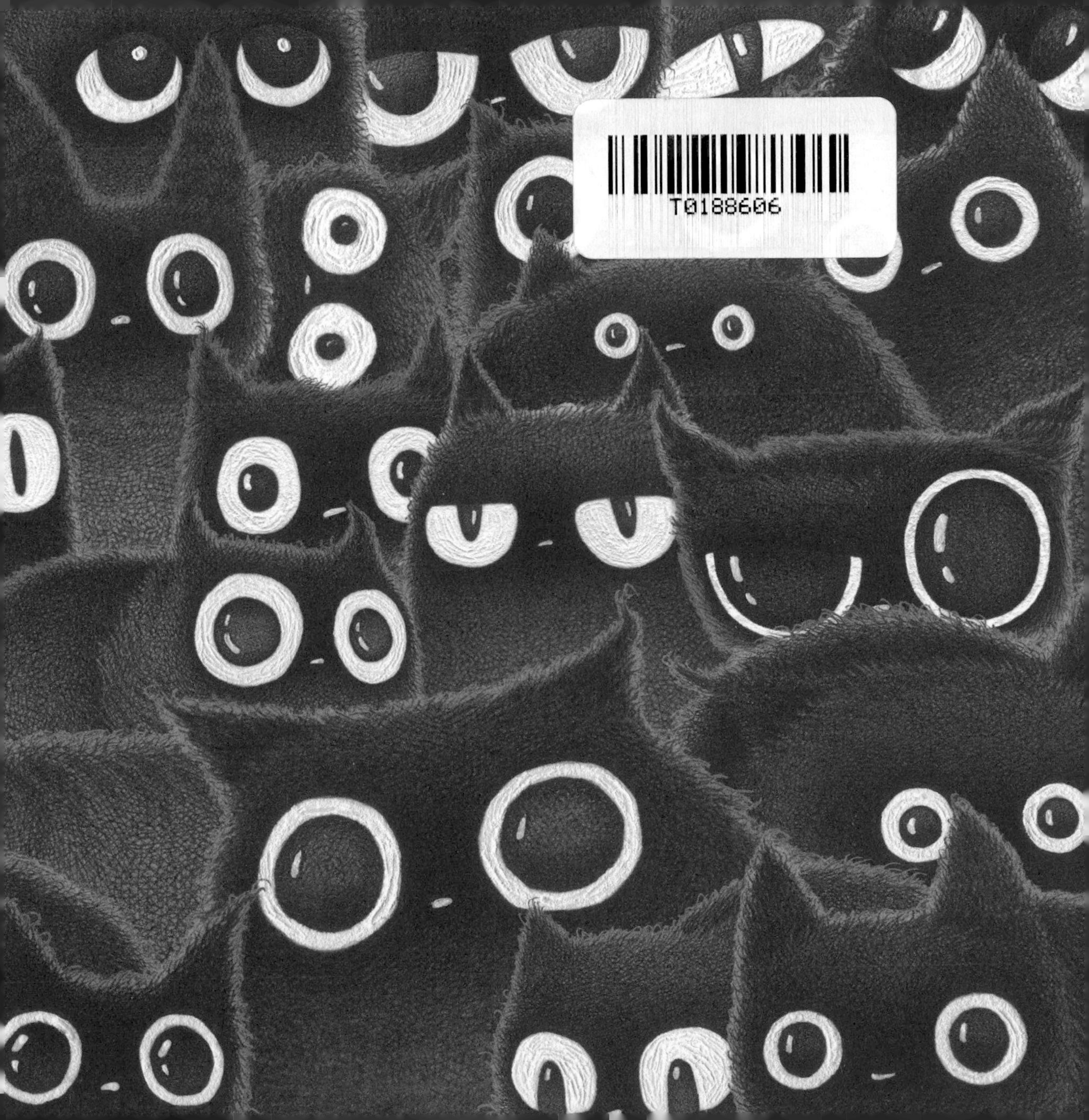

THE BOOK OF PURRS

everyday thoughts from
your feline friends

Luis Coelho

Andrews McMeel
PUBLISHING®

iNTRODUCTiON

Welcome to *The Book of Purrs*, a book that, much like cats, doesn't follow any rules. You don't need to read it in any particular order. Simply open it on any page and a friendly cat will be there, ready to share a message with you.

Each page is crafted to speak to you in the moment. Sometimes, you might find a funny cat joke. Other times, you could discover a comforting meow or a bit of feline wisdom that makes you think more deeply—or perhaps not think at all. But most importantly, this book will always try to make you smile.

Within these pages, you'll find a selection of my favorite comics, ones I've lovingly crafted and shared online over the years, as well as brand-new ones, making their debut right here. Alongside some characters that you might have seen online, you'll also meet thirty cats that I've specially drawn for this book.

I've poured my heart and soul into creating this book, my very first, and I truly hope it becomes a cherished companion for those moments when you need a little brightness in your day.

Thank you for joining me on this journey of laughter, comfort, and the simple yet profound lessons our feline friends offer.

May the purr be with you,

Luis

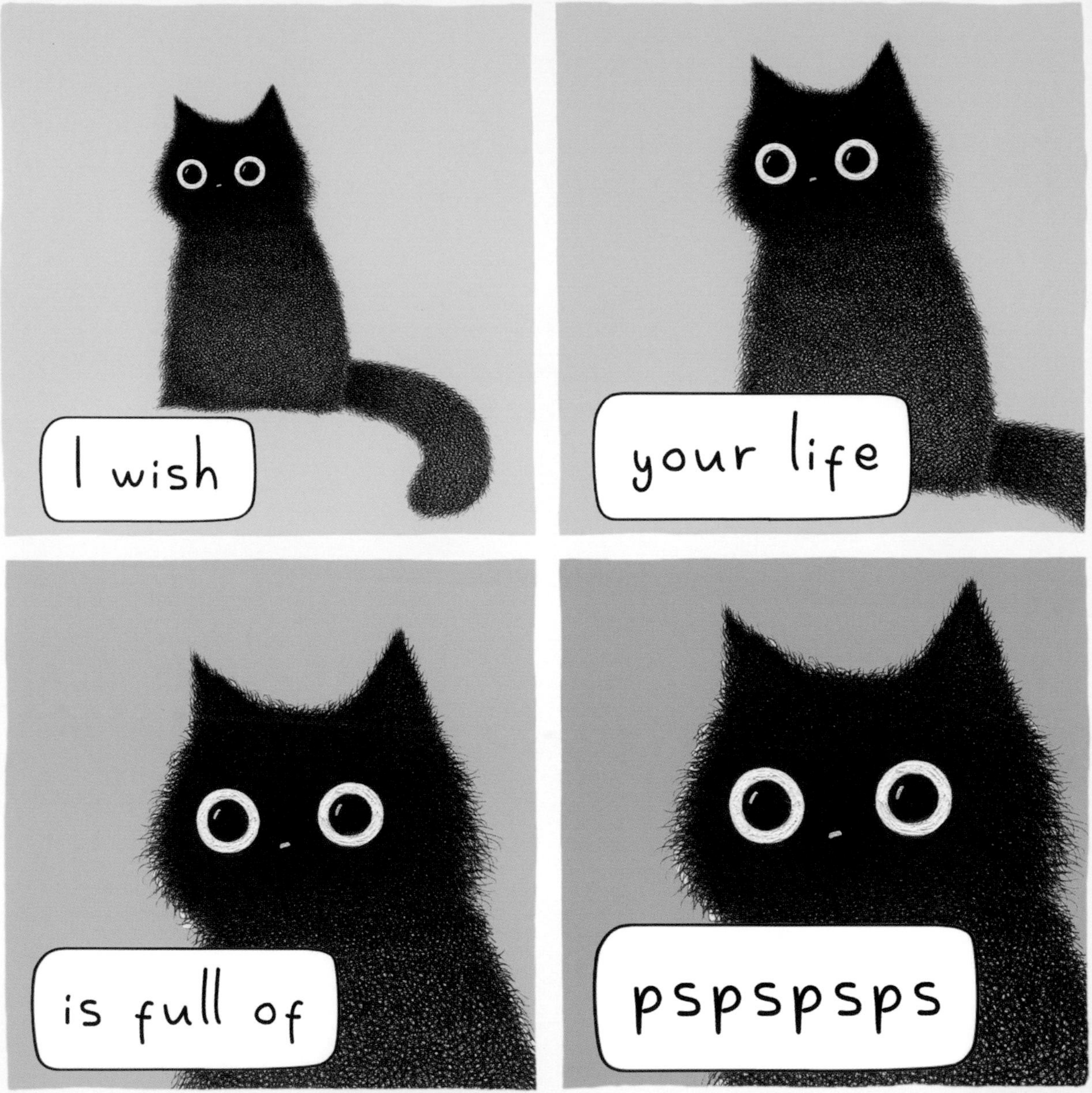
I wish
your life
is full of
pspspsps

By the power of the purr
and the beauty of the fur
good things will occur

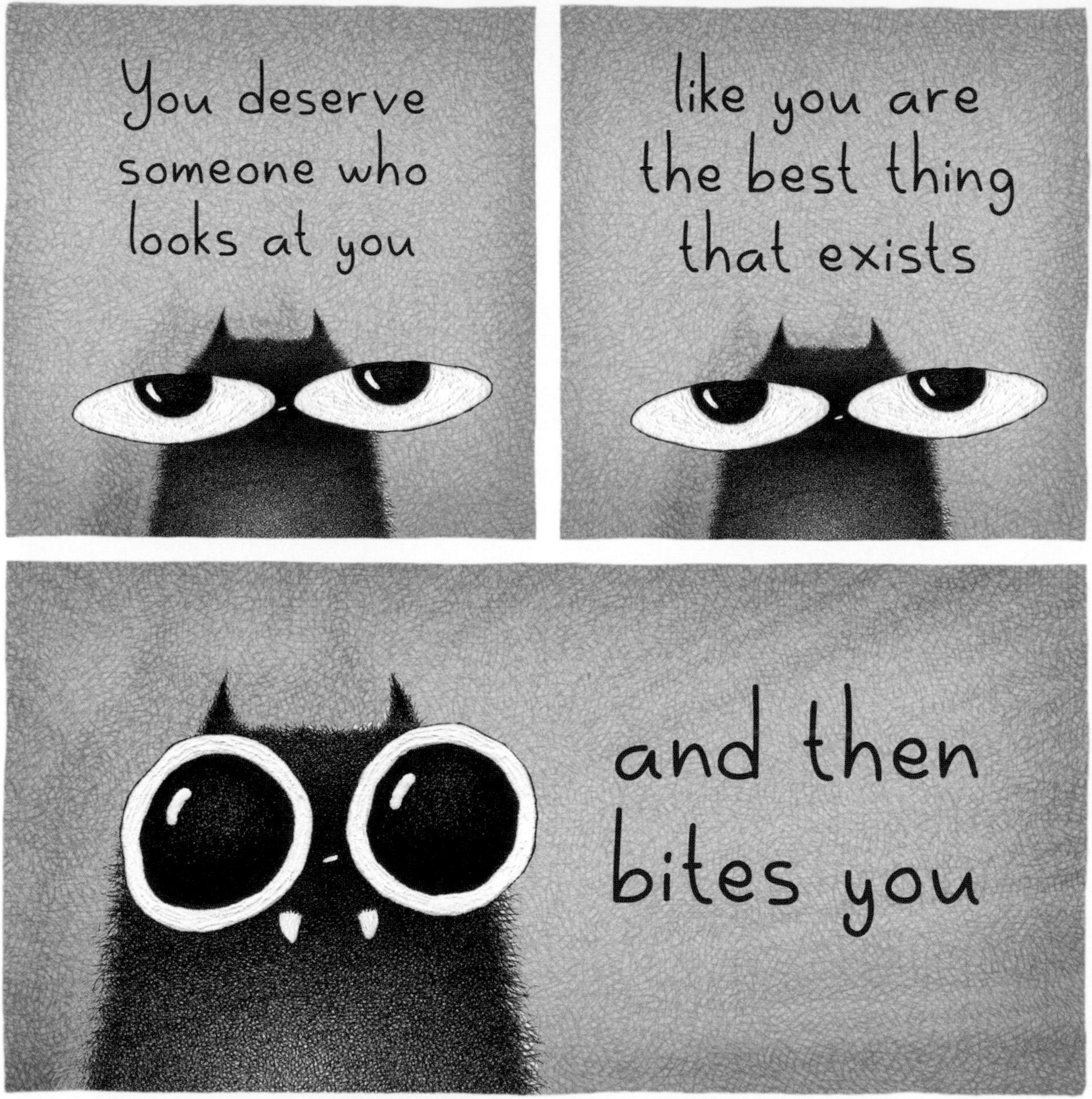
You deserve someone who looks at you
like you are the best thing that exists
and then bites you

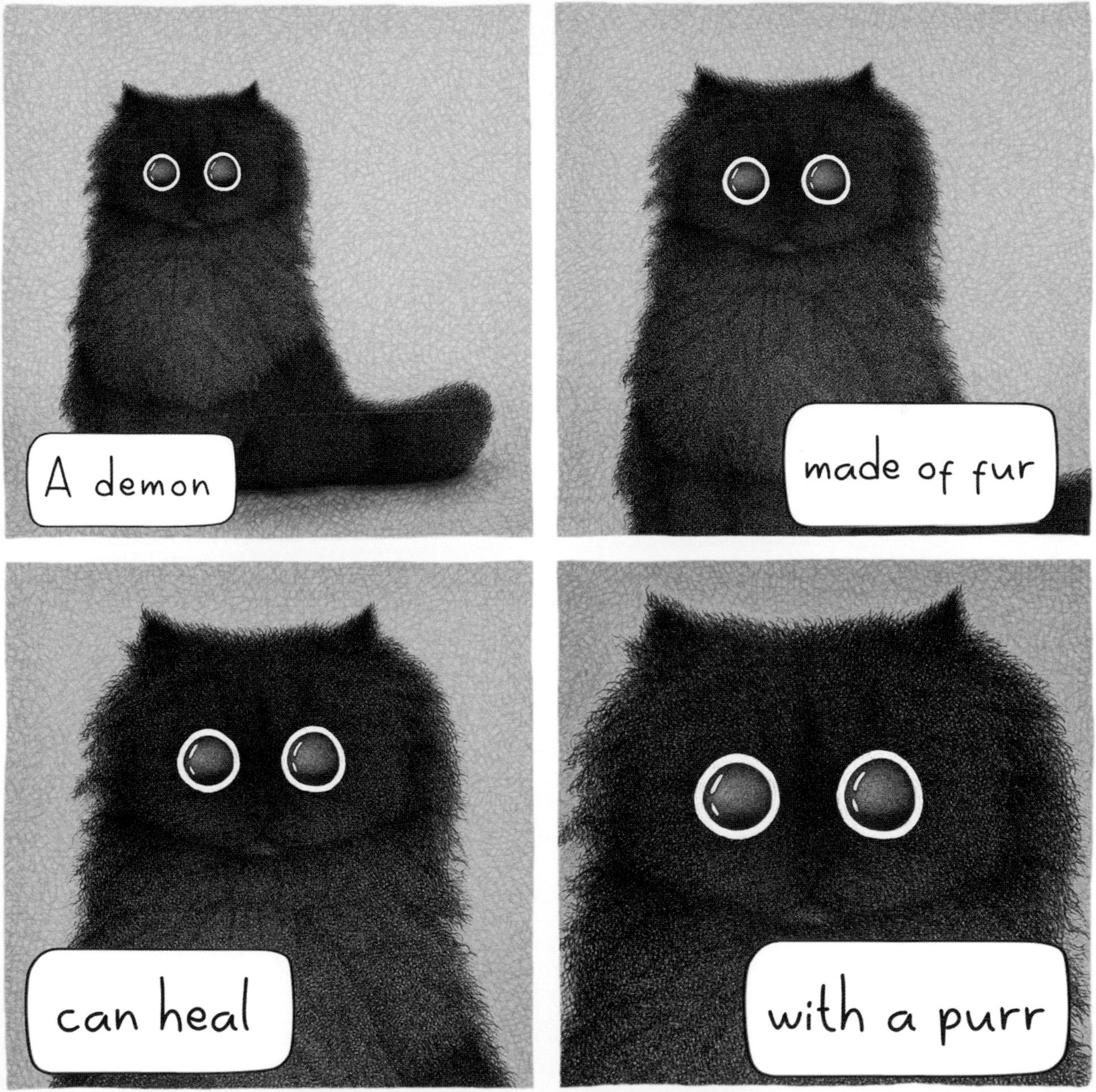
A demon
made of fur
can heal
with a purr

Two wonderful beings
looking at each other

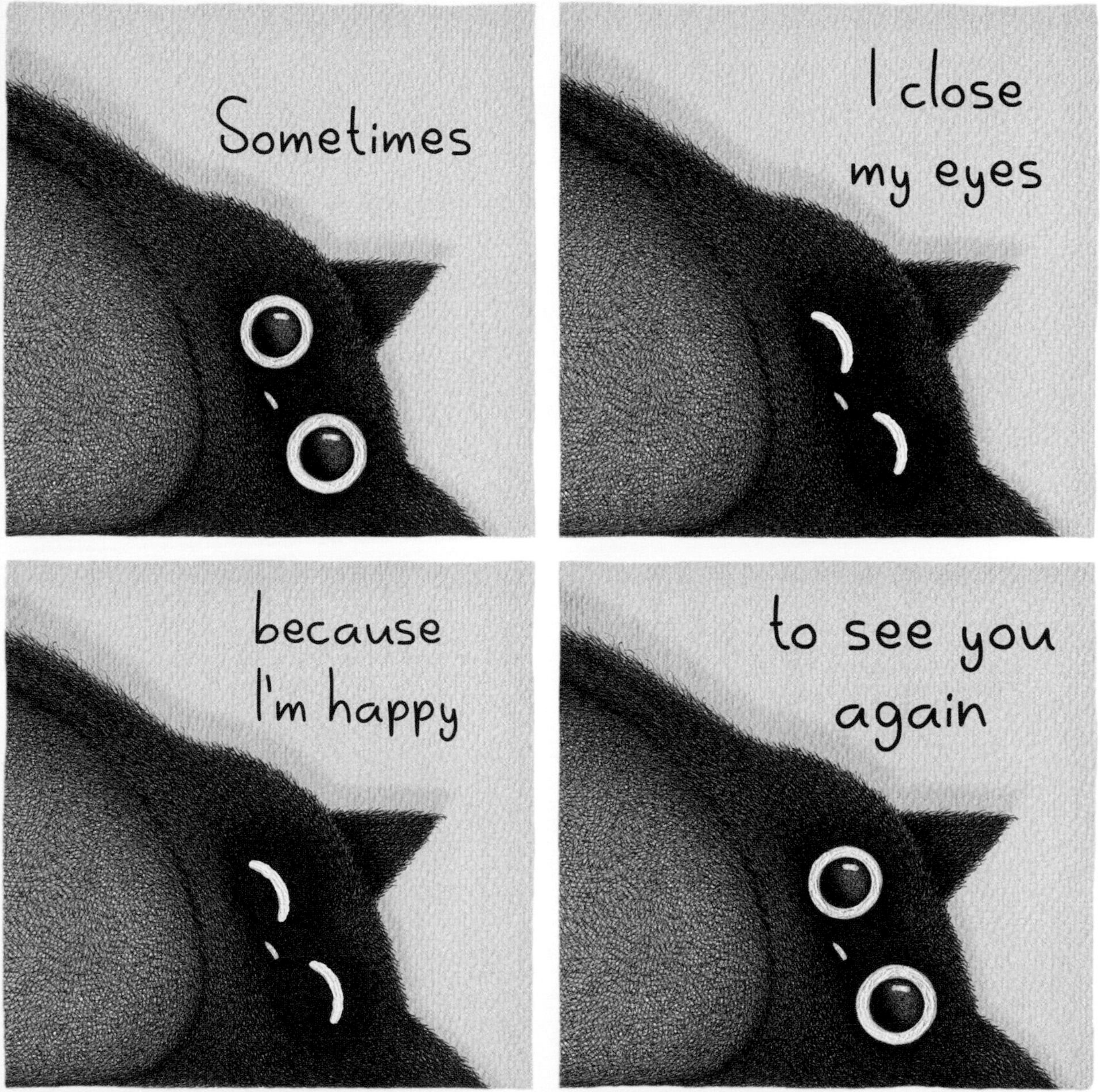
Sometimes
I close my eyes
because I'm happy
to see you again

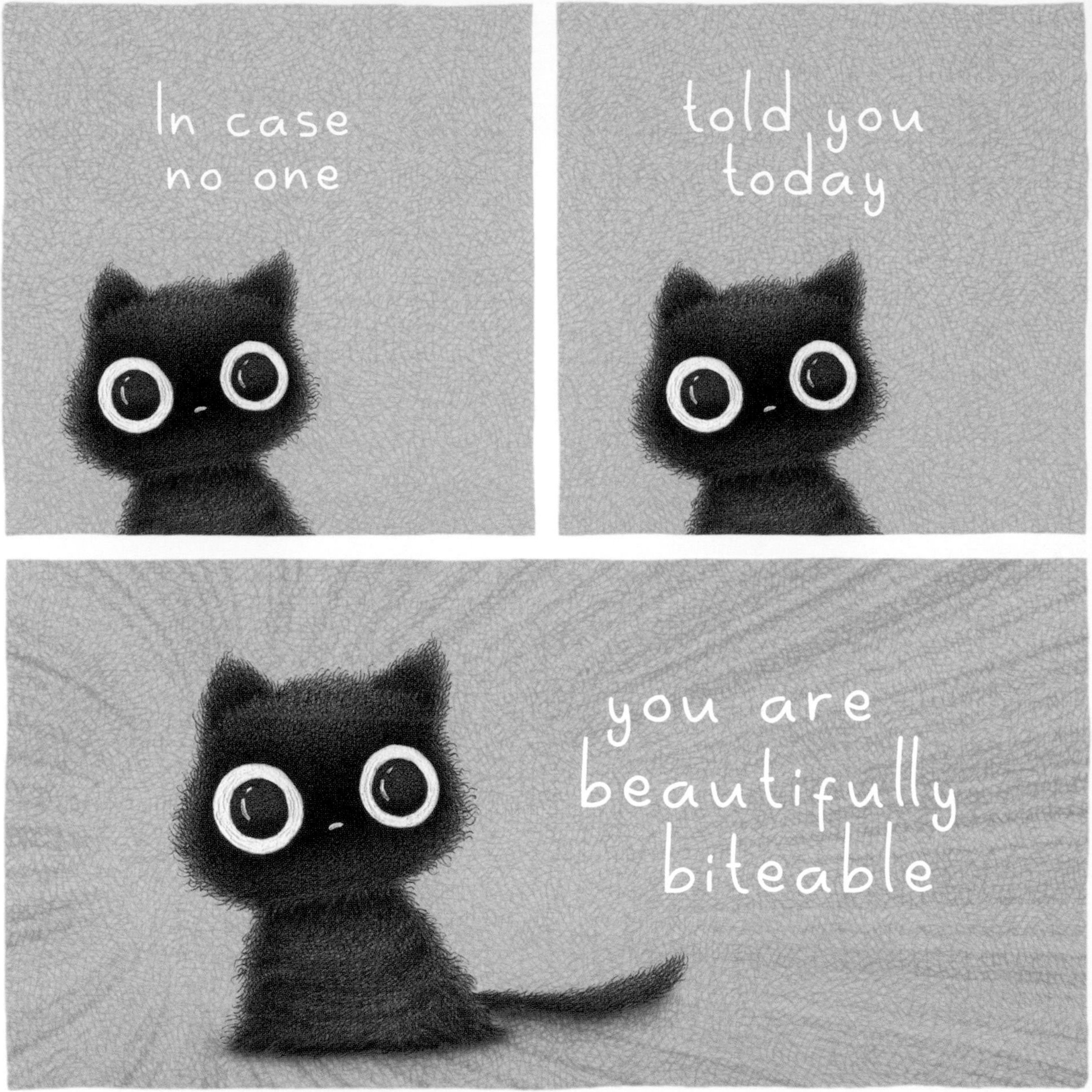
In case
no one
told you
today
you are
beautifully
biteable

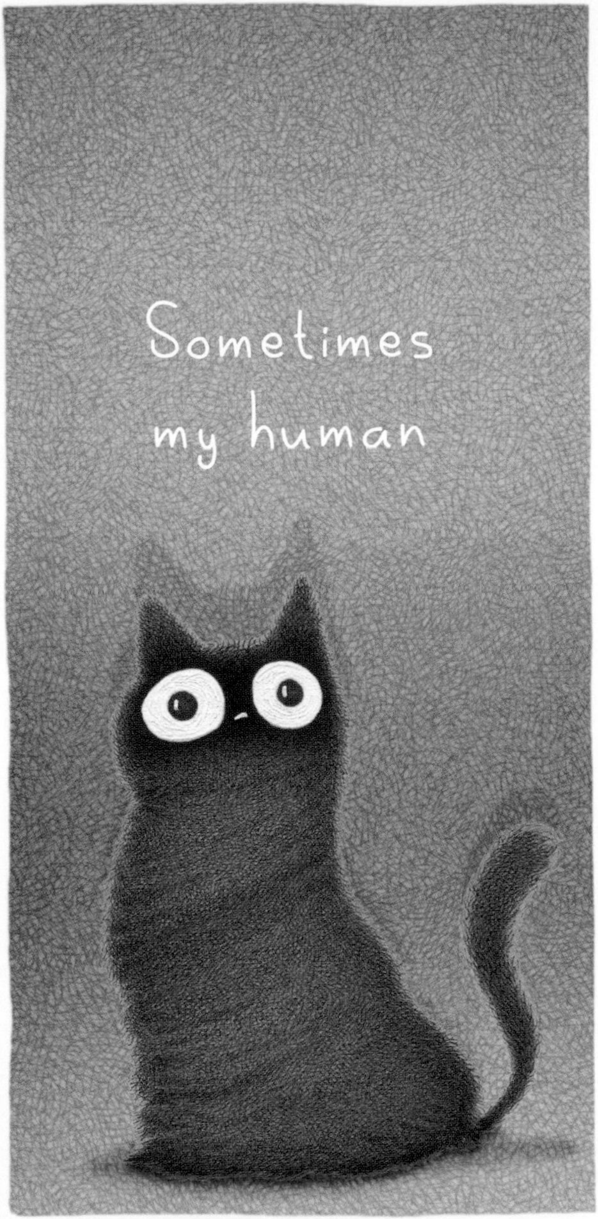
Sometimes
my human
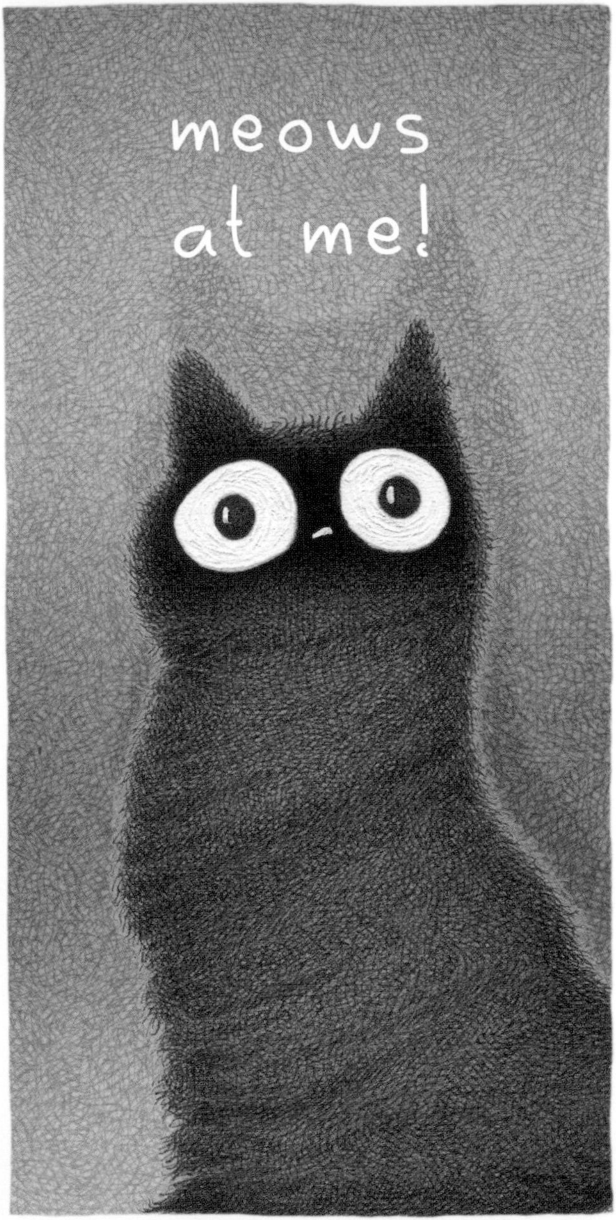
meows
at me!

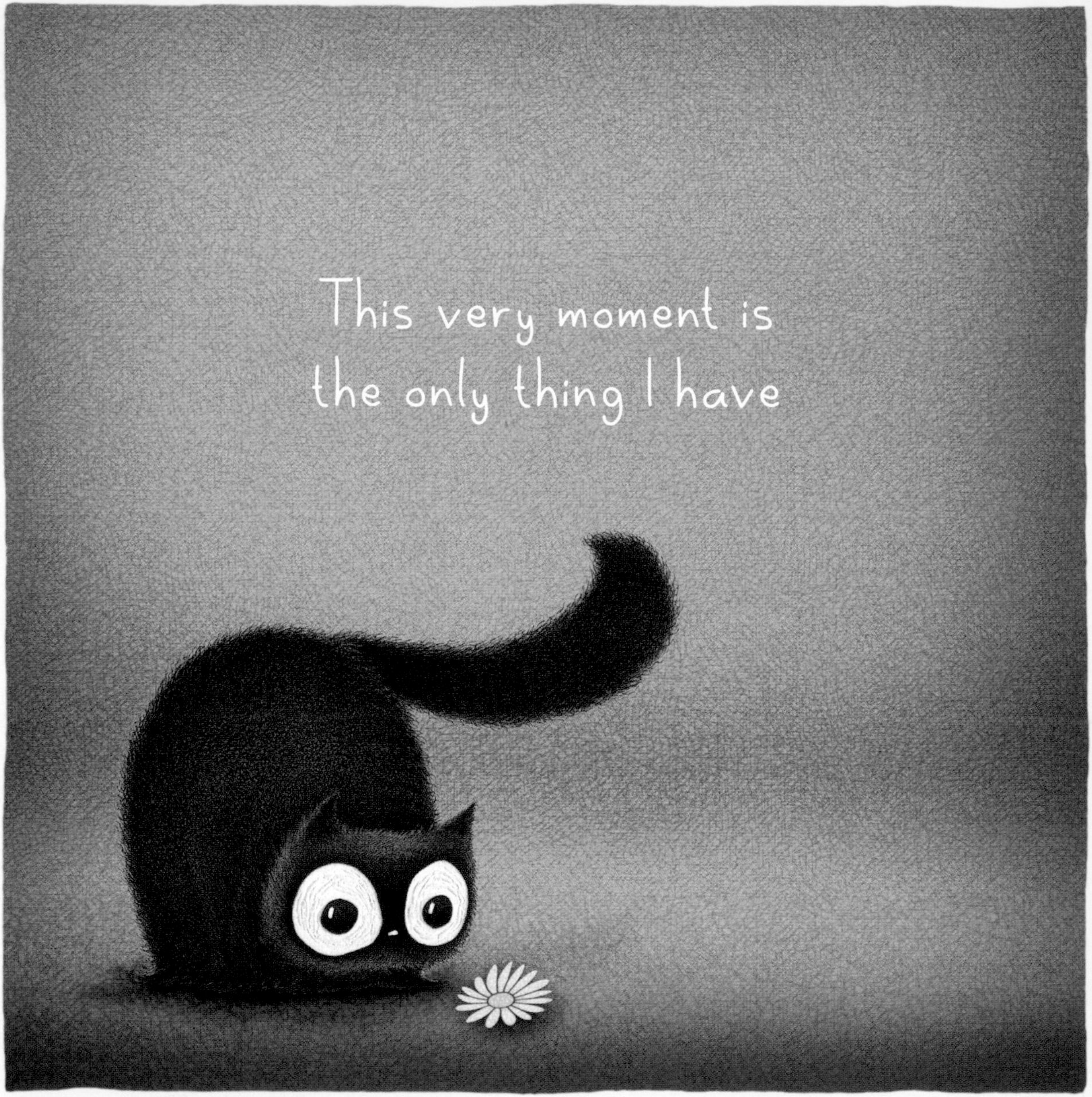
This very moment is
the only thing I have

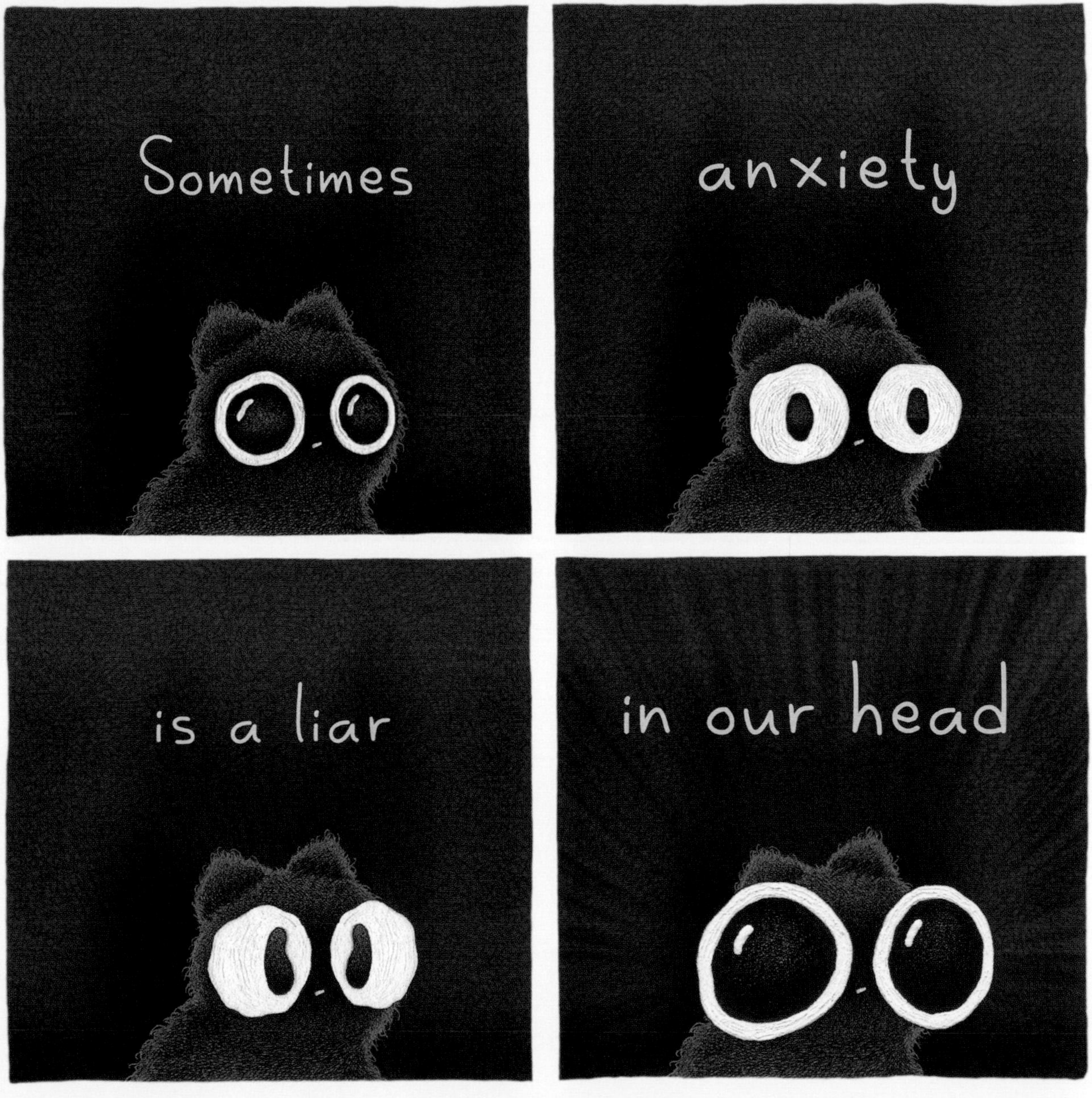
Sometimes
anxiety
is a liar
in our head

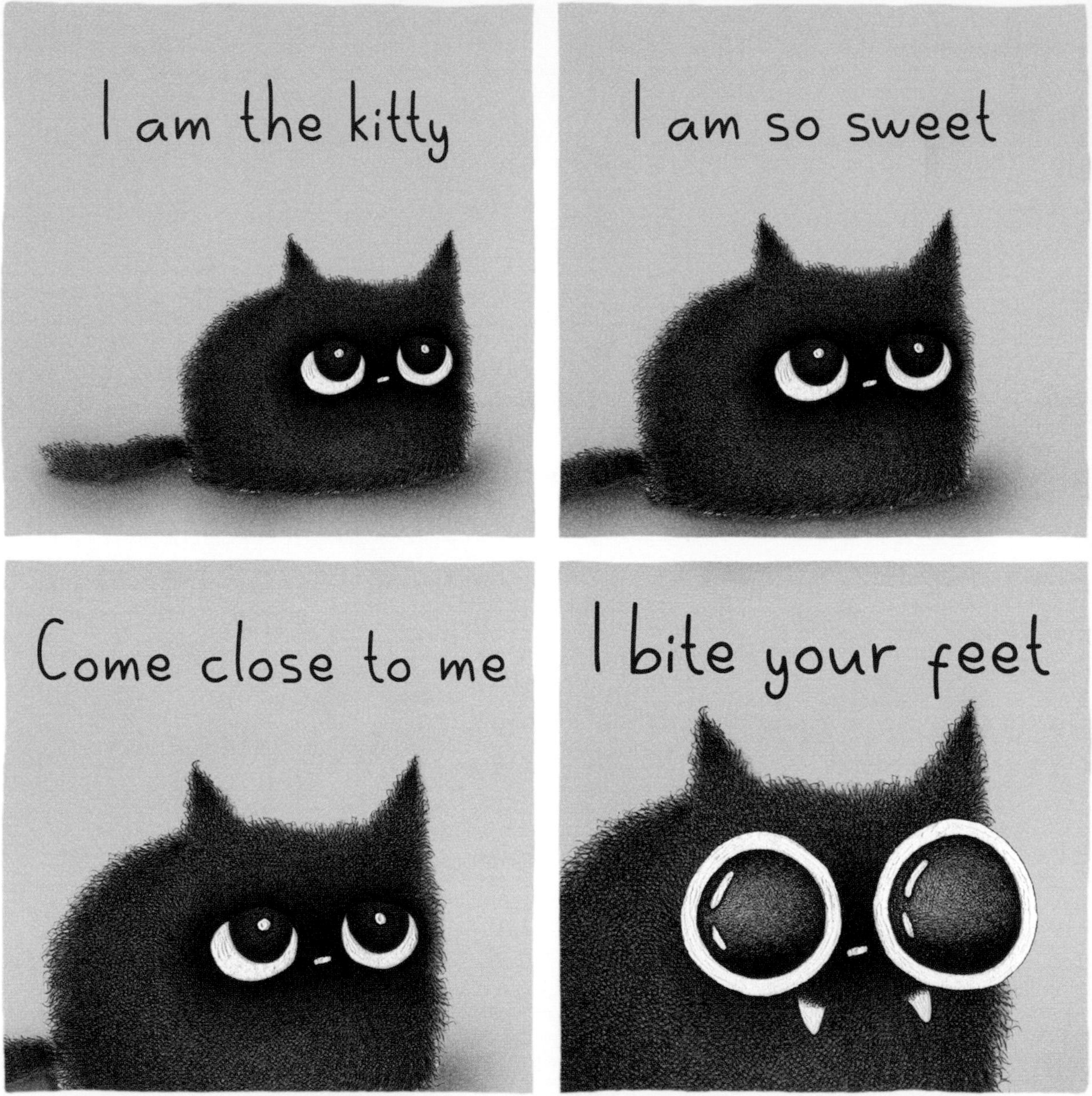
I am the kitty
I am so sweet
Come close to me
I bite your feet

Every bite is a love bite
when you love bites

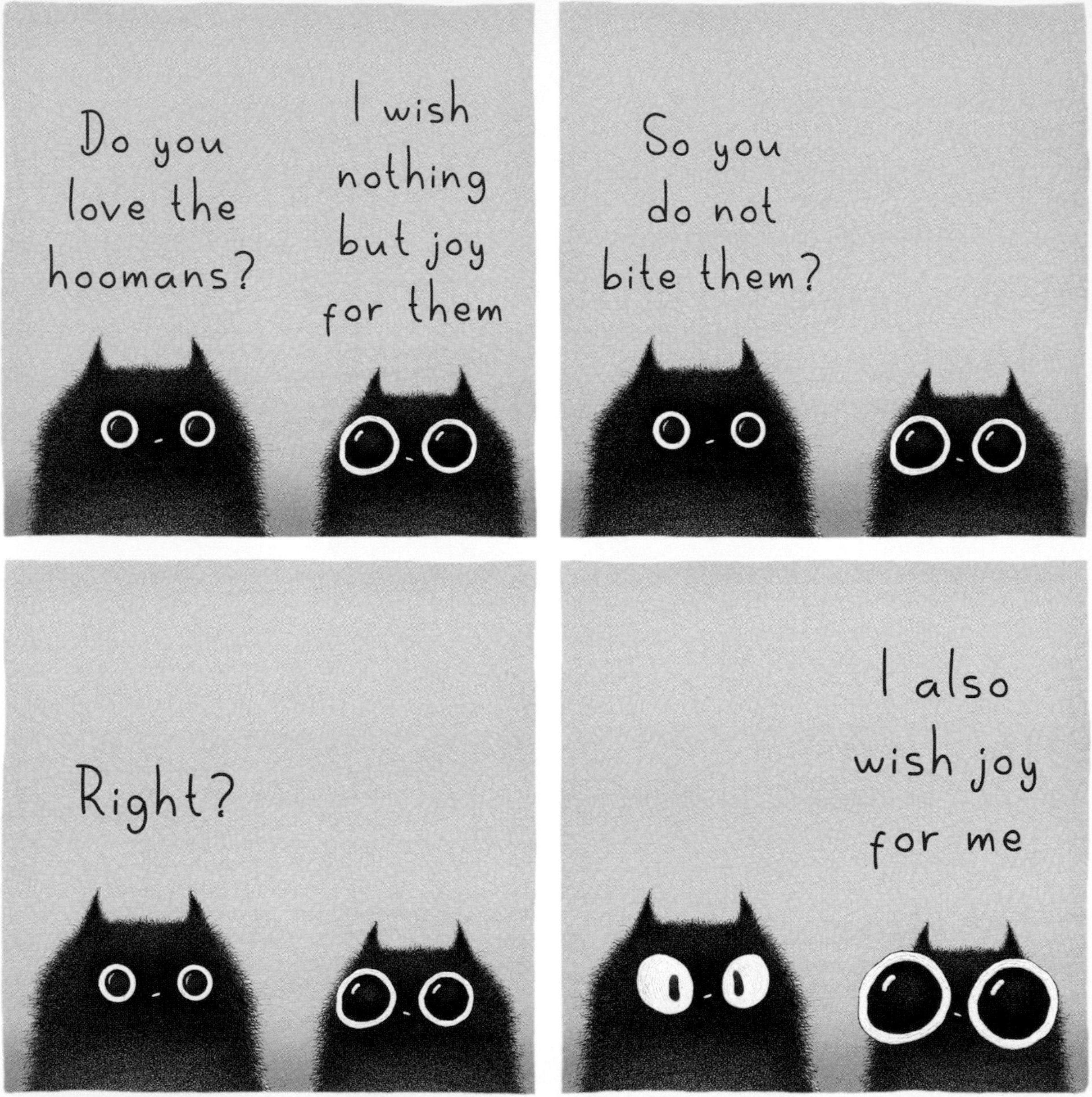
Do you love the hoomans?
I wish nothing but joy for them
So you do not bite them?
Right?
I also wish joy for me

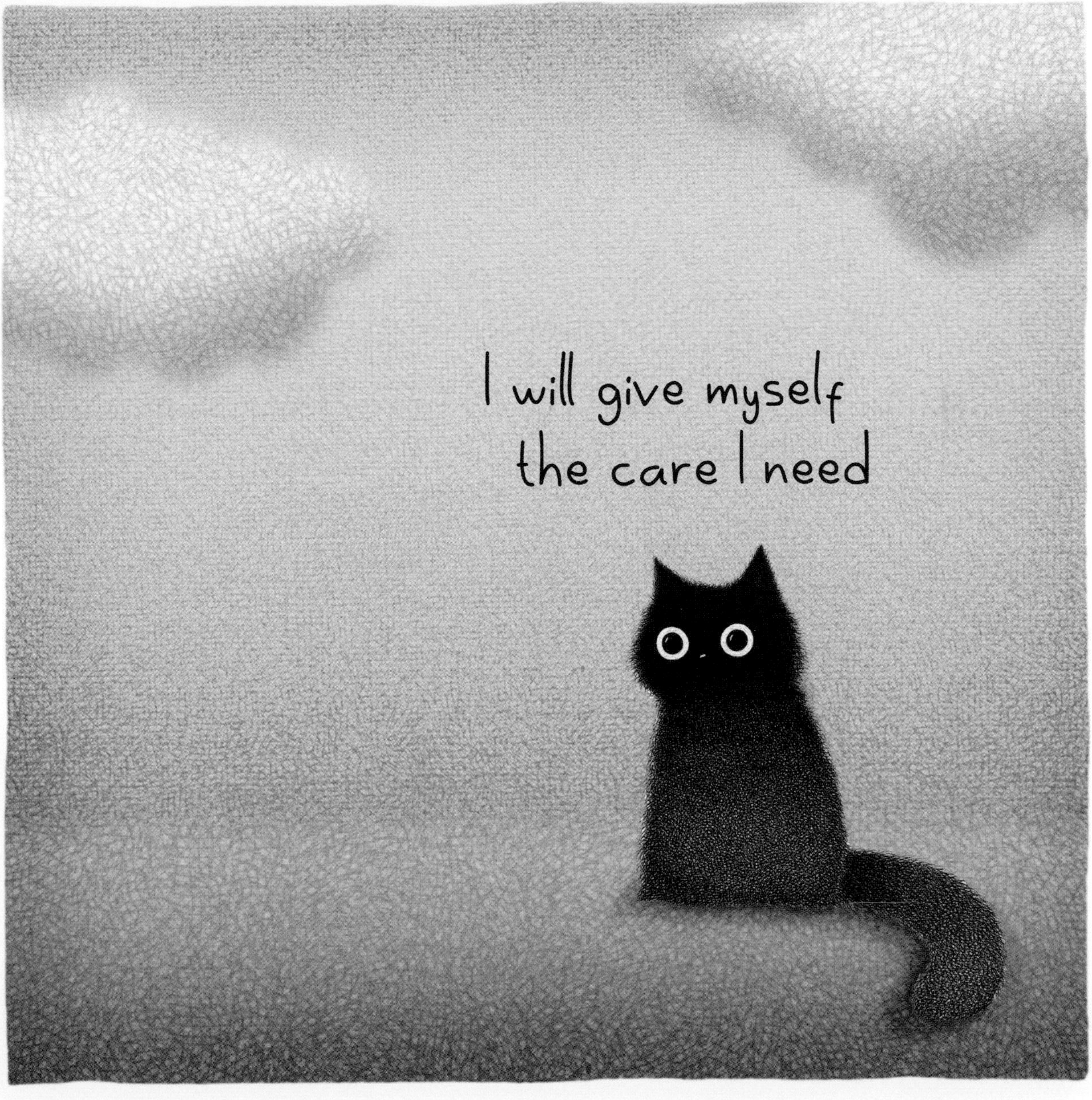
I will give myself
the care I need

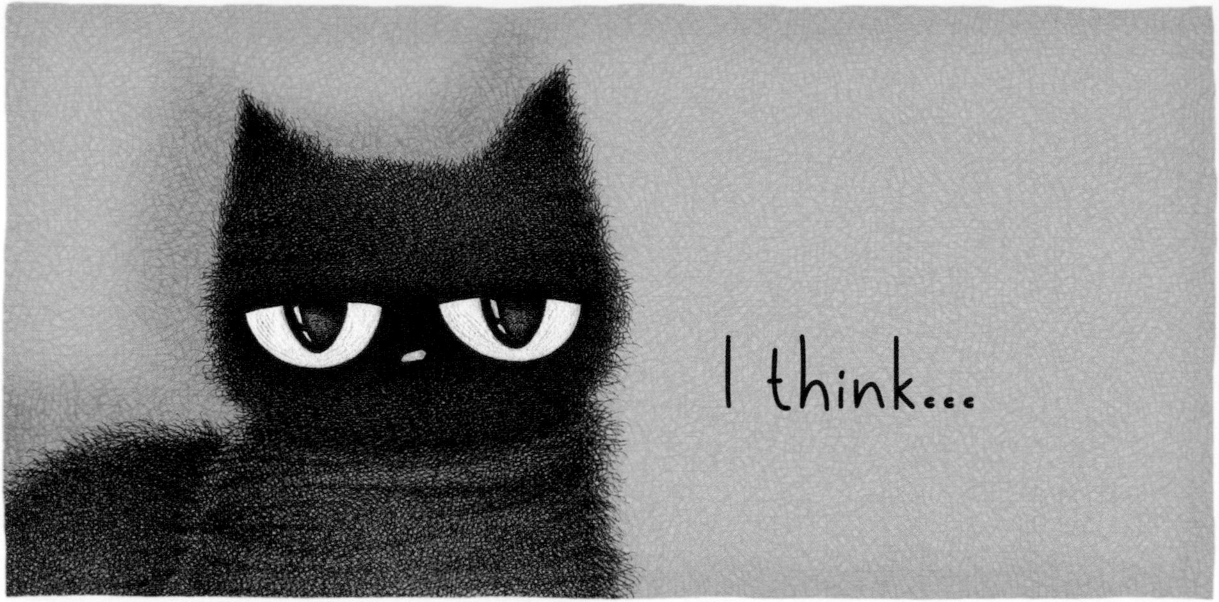
I think...

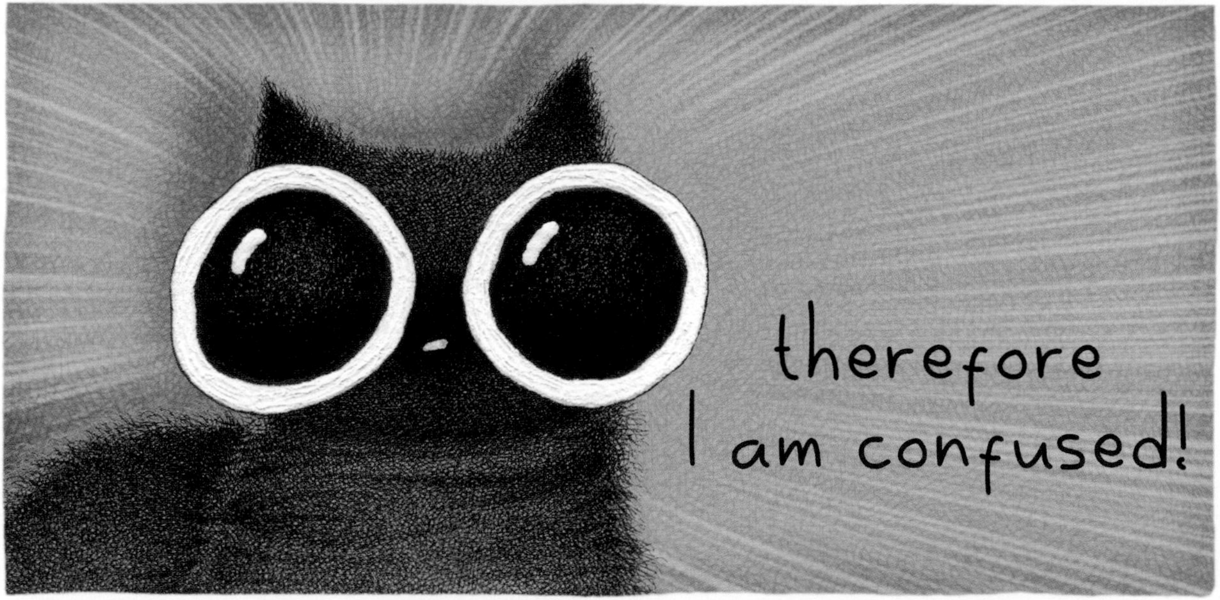
therefore
I am confused!

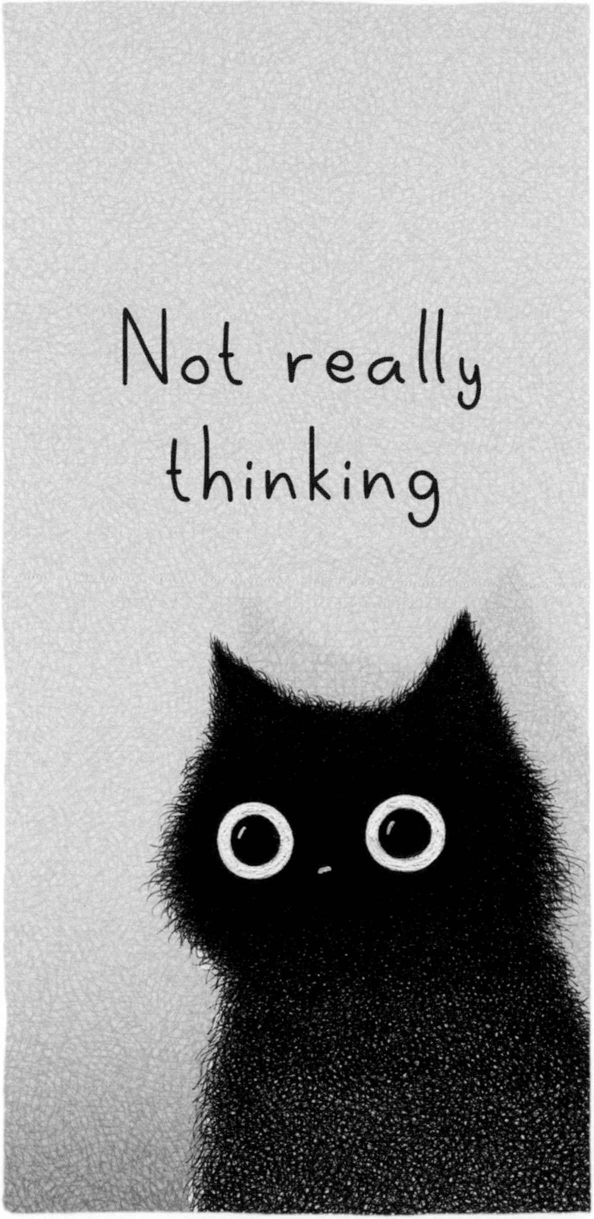
Not really thinking

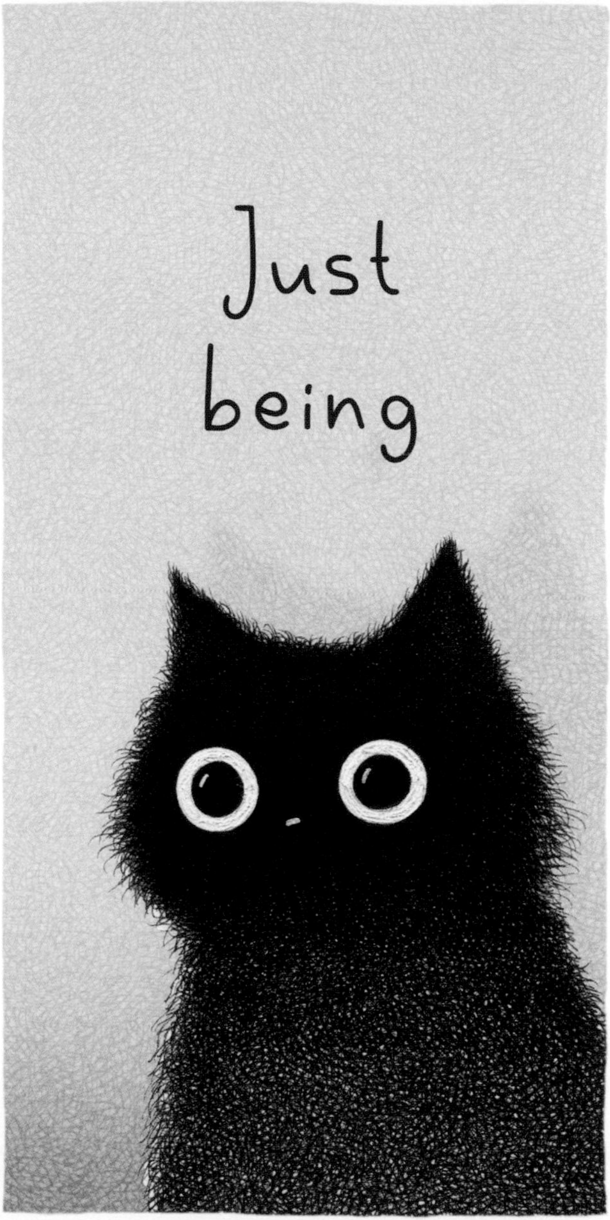
Just being

IN THE HERE
IN THE NOW
NO WORRIES
ONLY MEOW

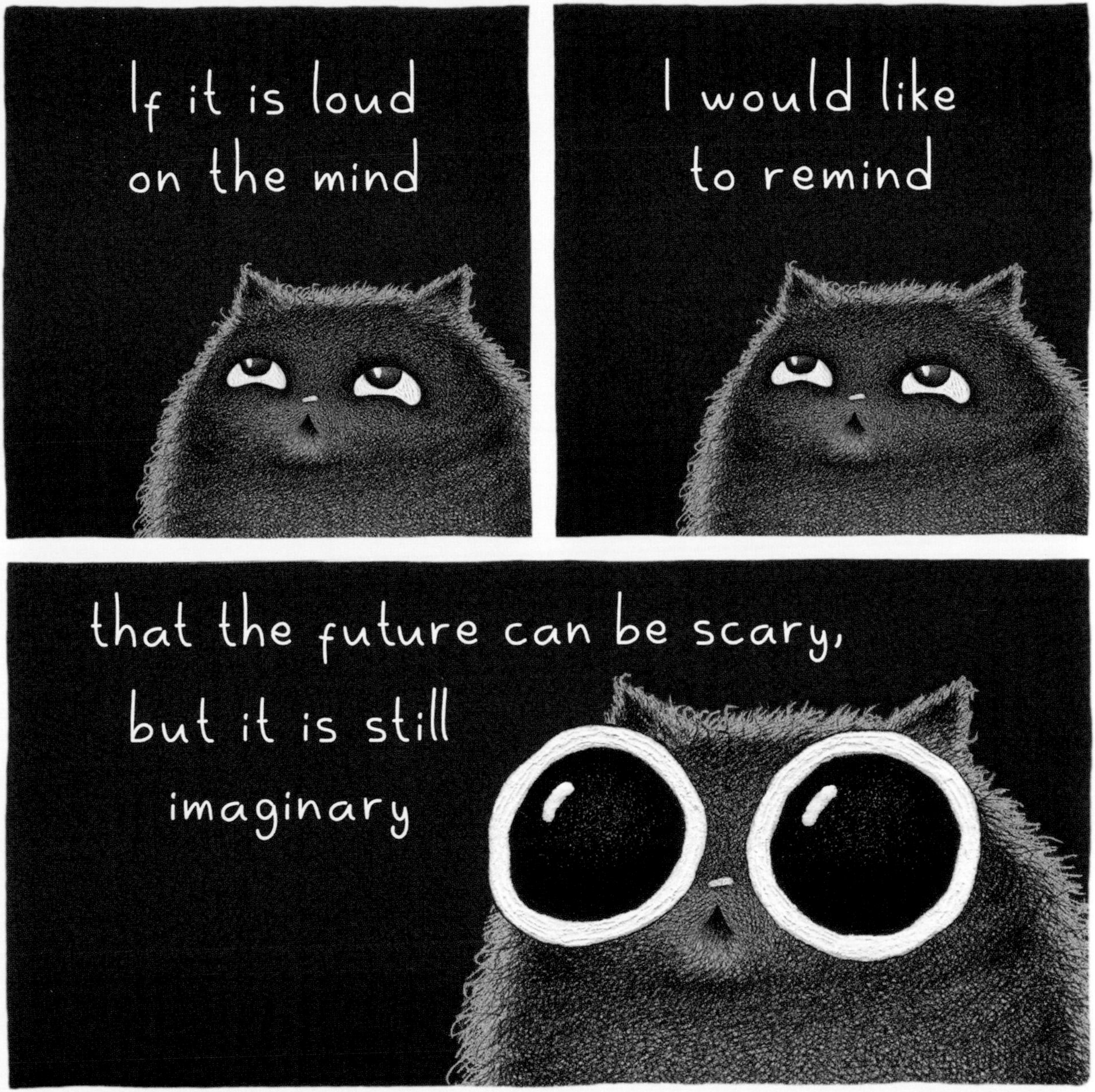
If it is loud
on the mind
I would like
to remind
that the future can be scary,
but it is still
imaginary

You give me home

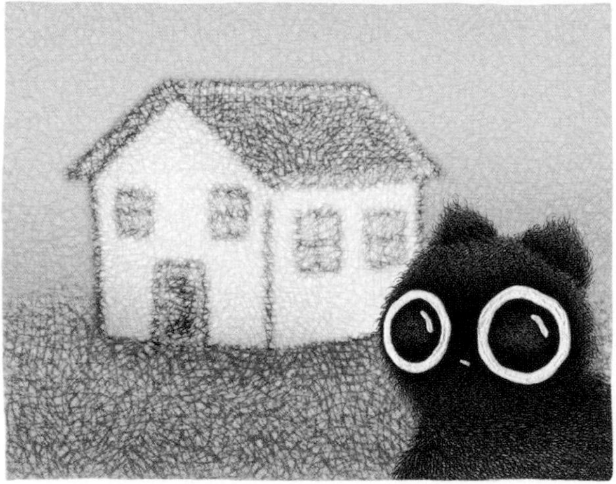

You give me meal

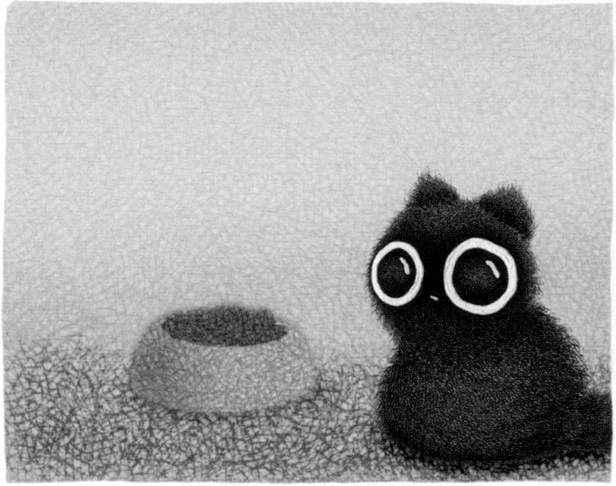

I give you purr to heal

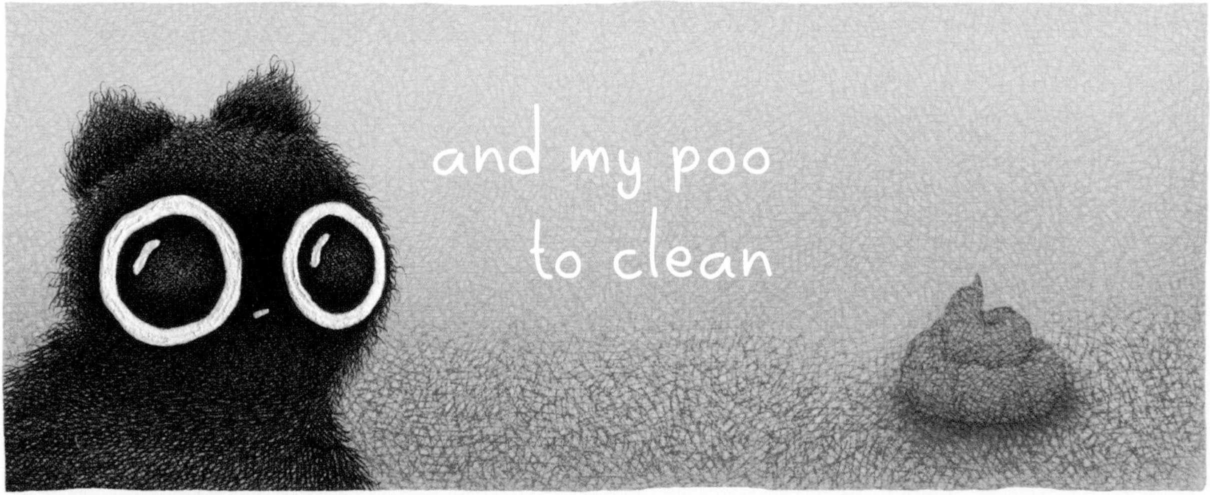
and my poo
to clean

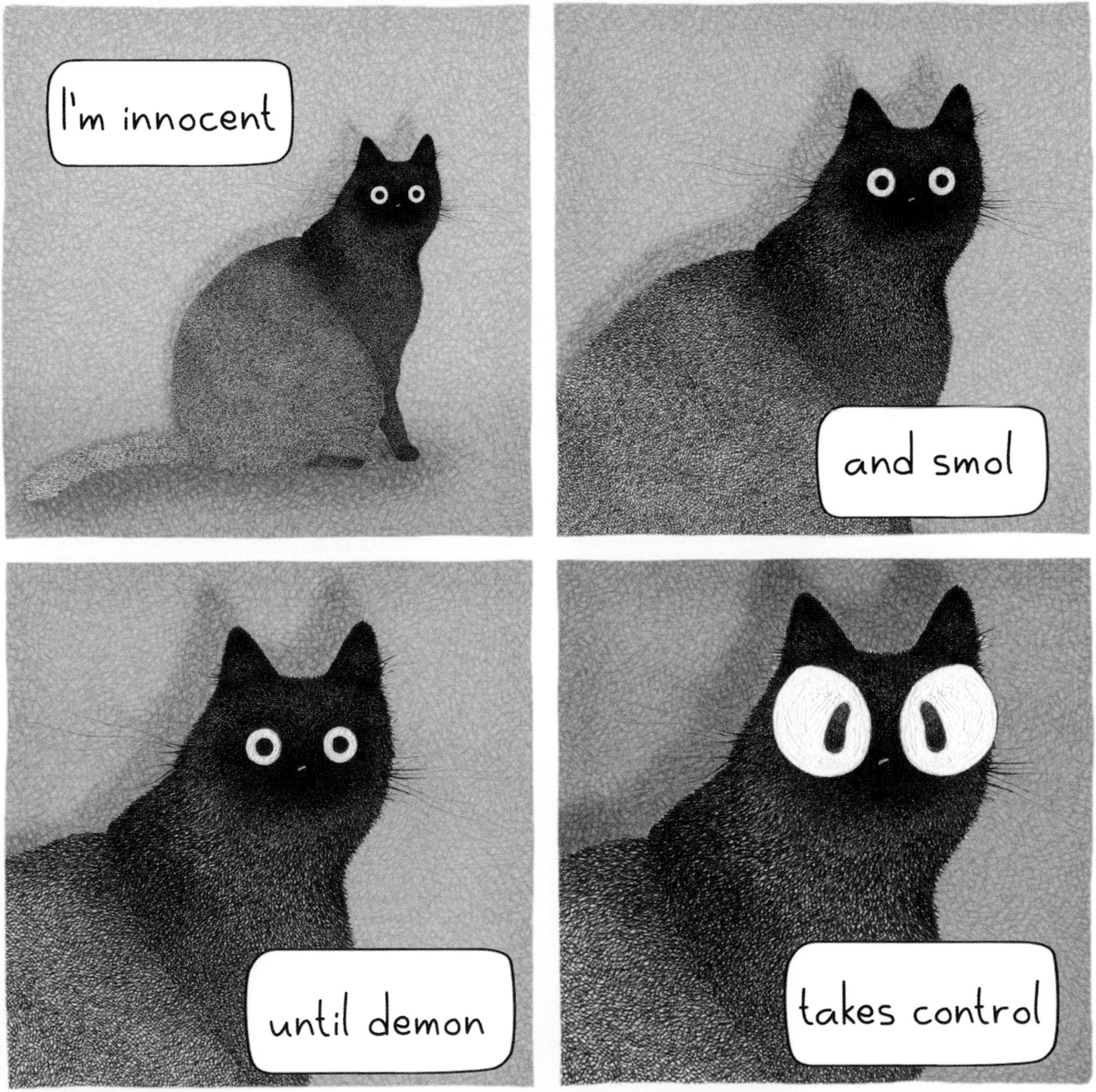
I'm innocent
and smol
until demon
takes control

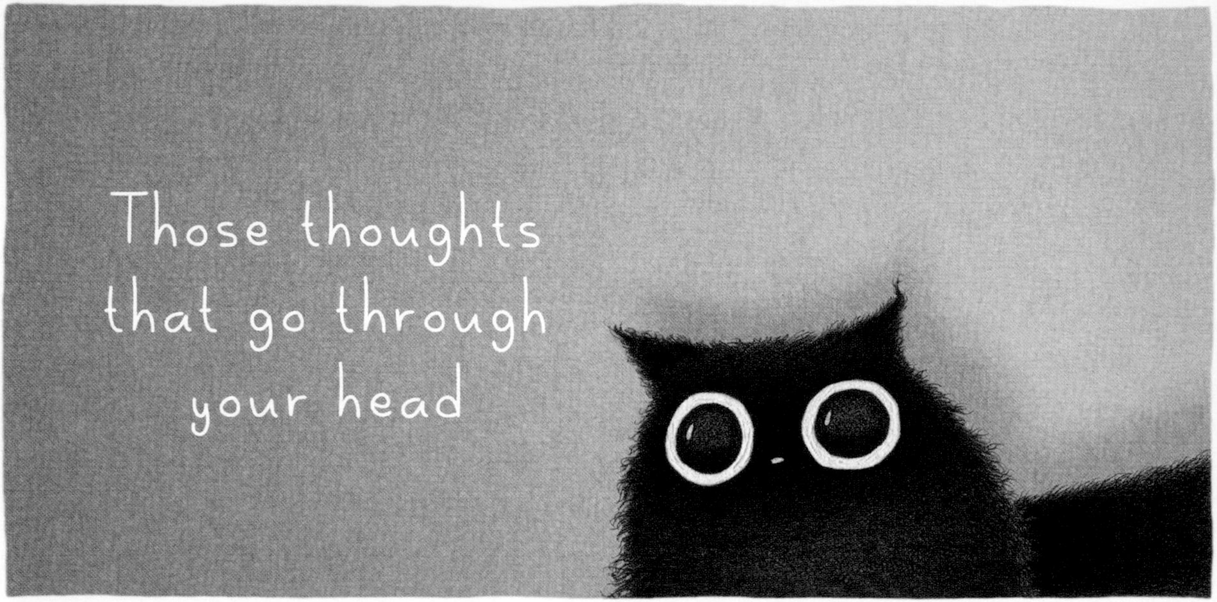
Those thoughts
that go through
your head

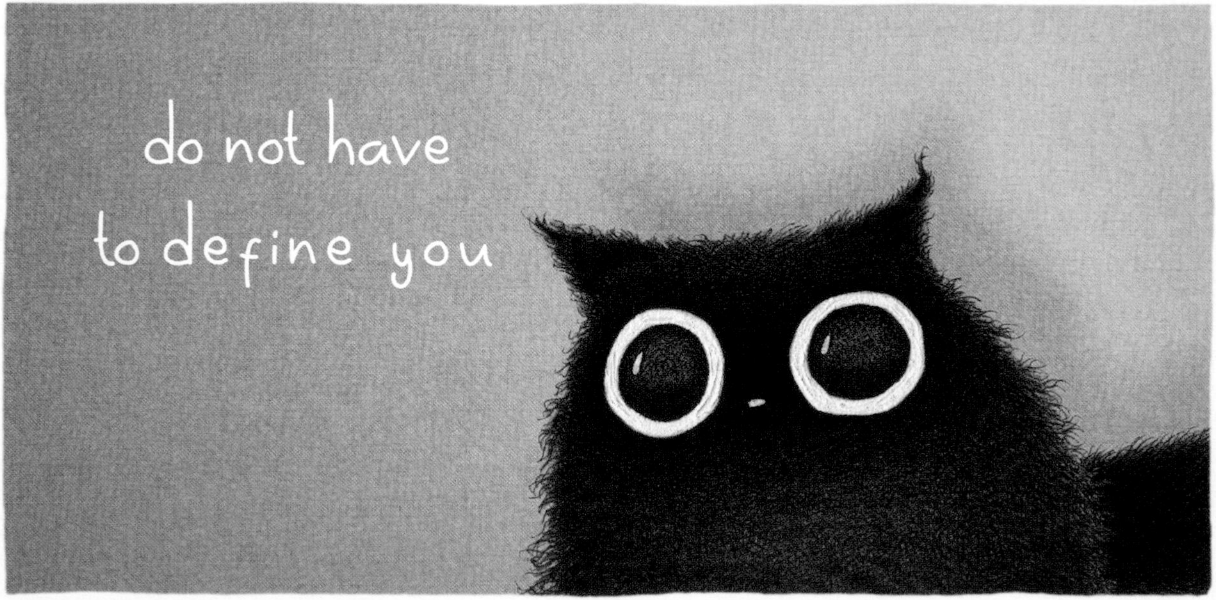
do not have
to define you

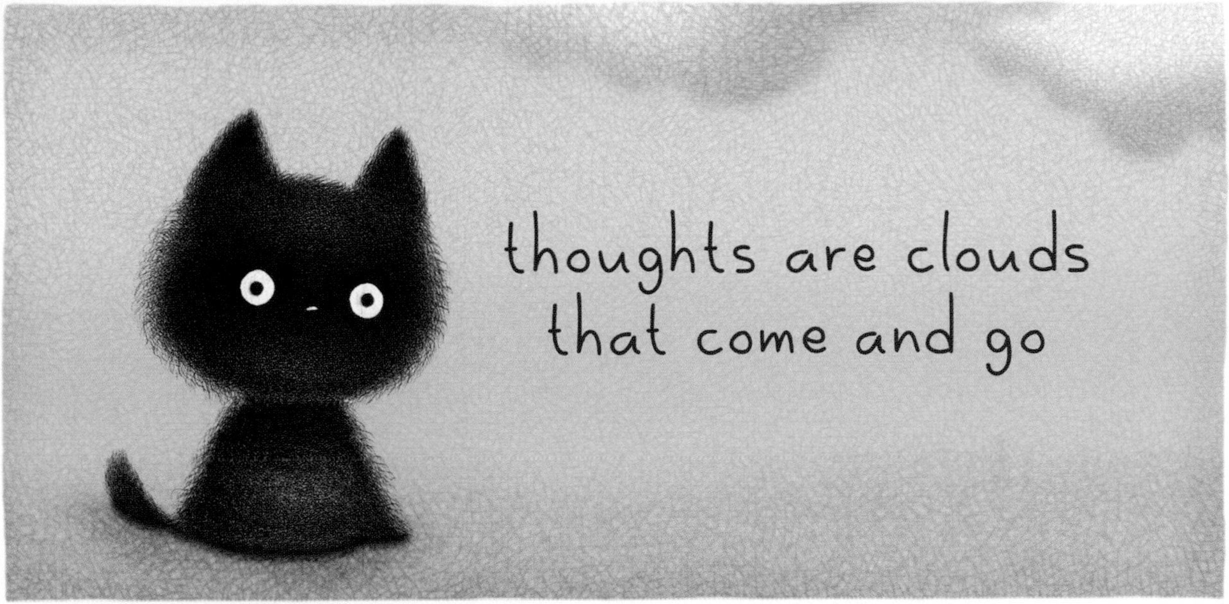
thoughts are clouds
that come and go

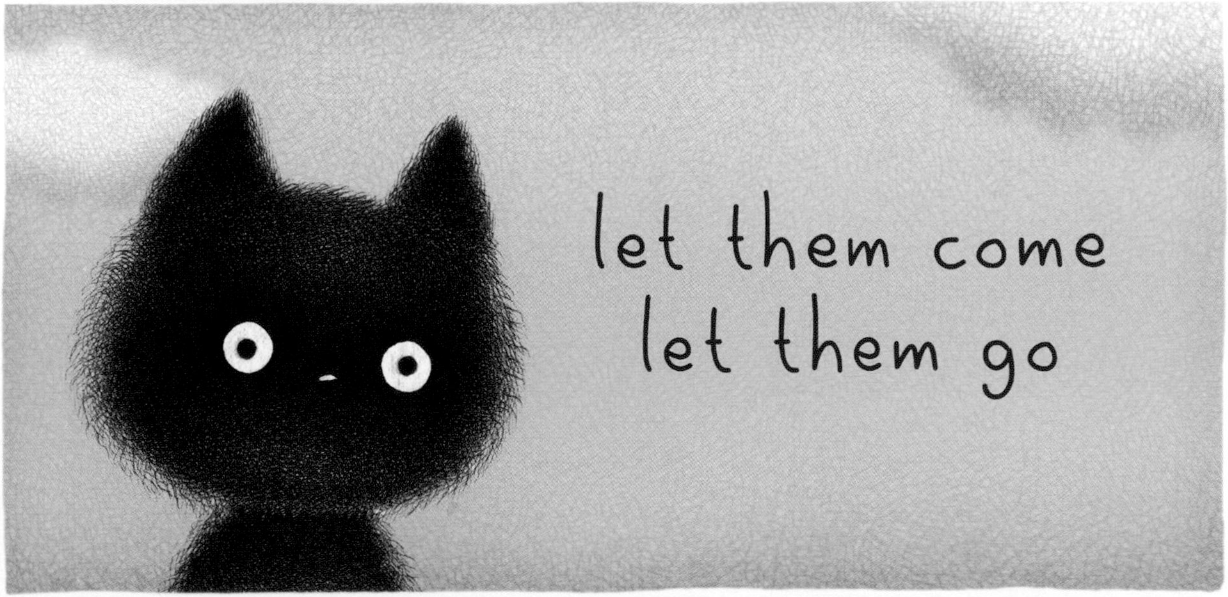
let them come
let them go

Sometimes we must cry
for our flowers to bloom

Some days
  you might feel ugly
and everything seems wrong

so we came here
      to tell you

you are beautiful and strong

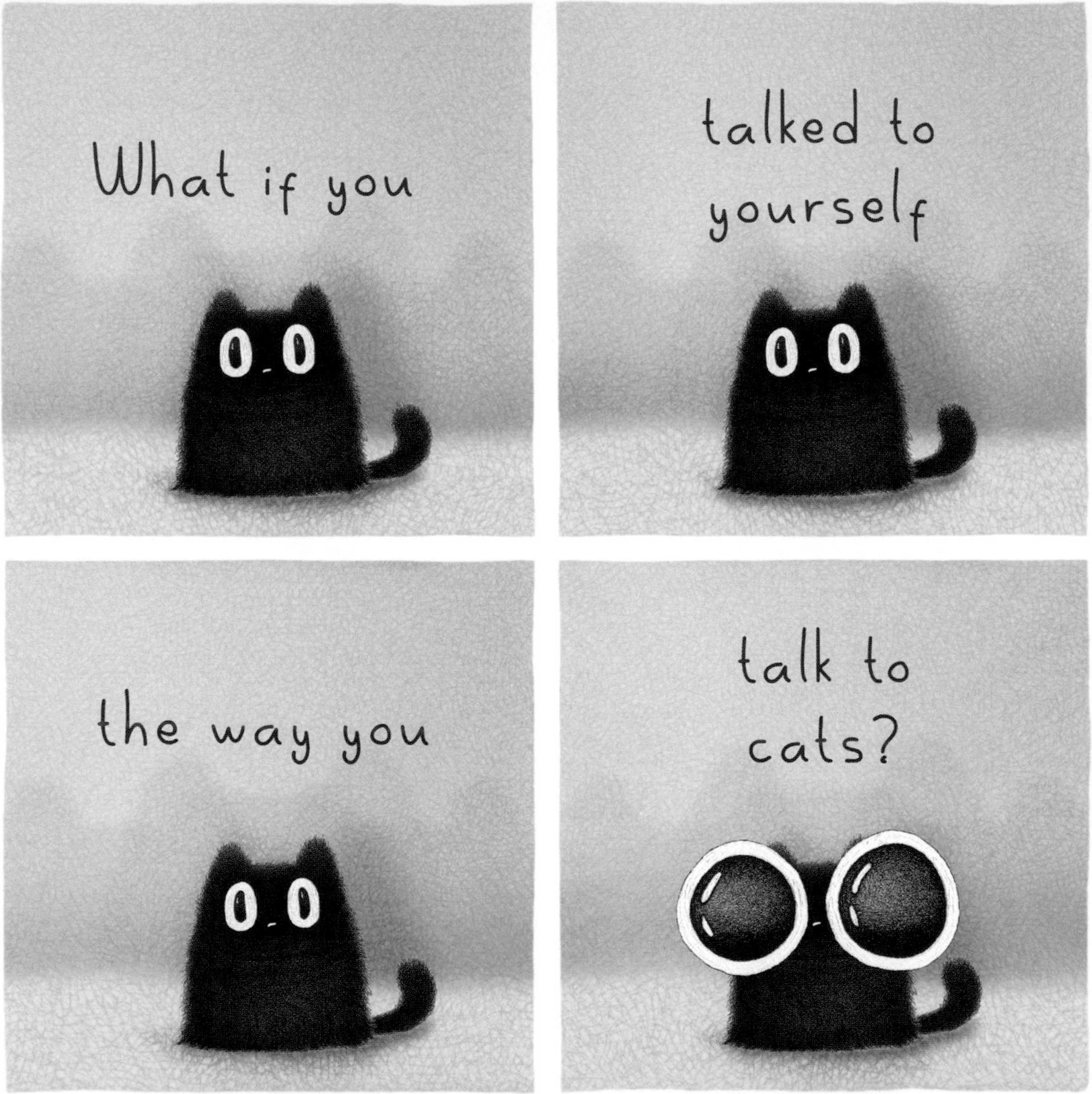
What if you
talked to yourself
the way you
talk to cats?

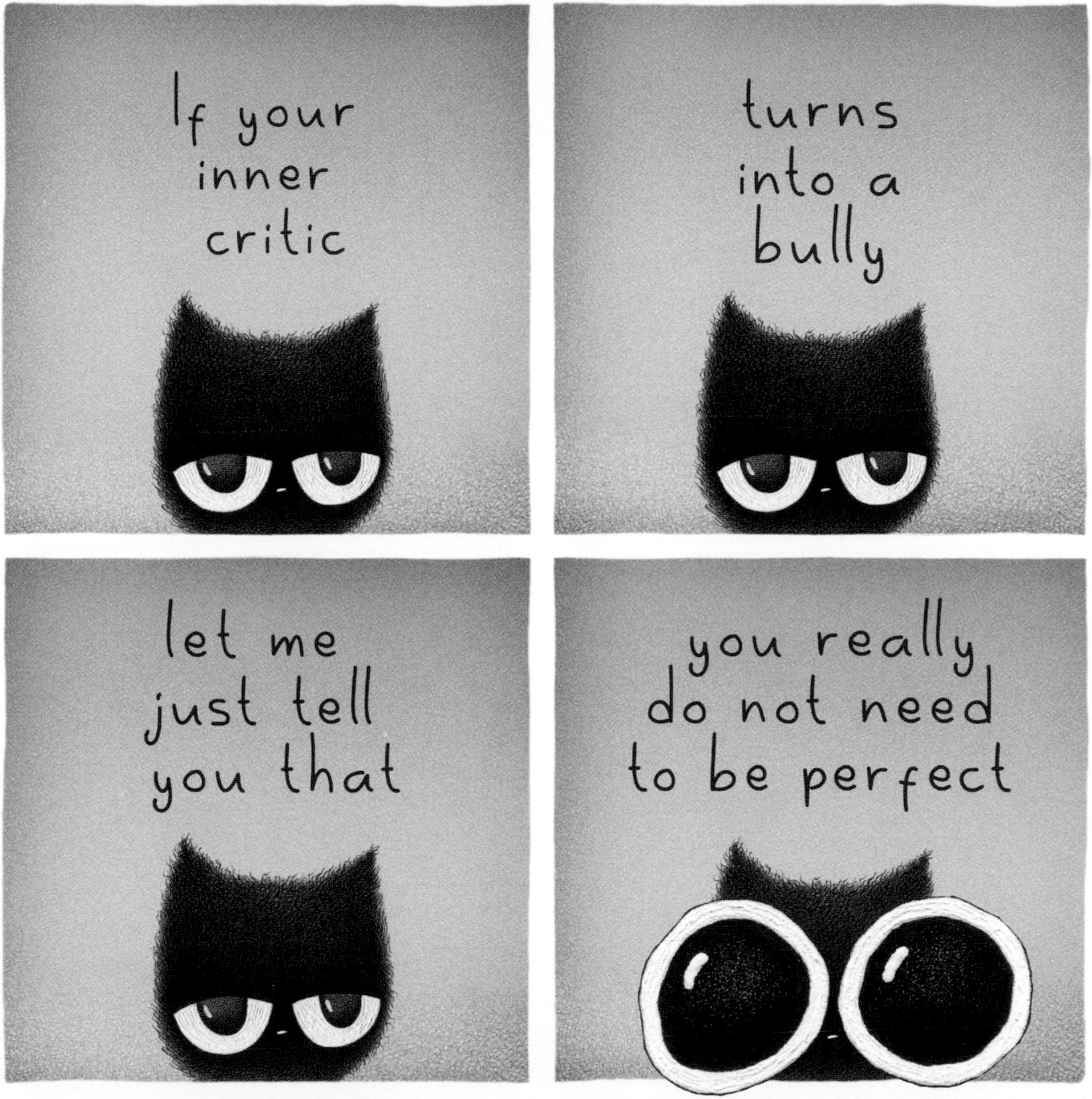
If your inner critic
turns into a bully
let me just tell you that
you really do not need to be perfect

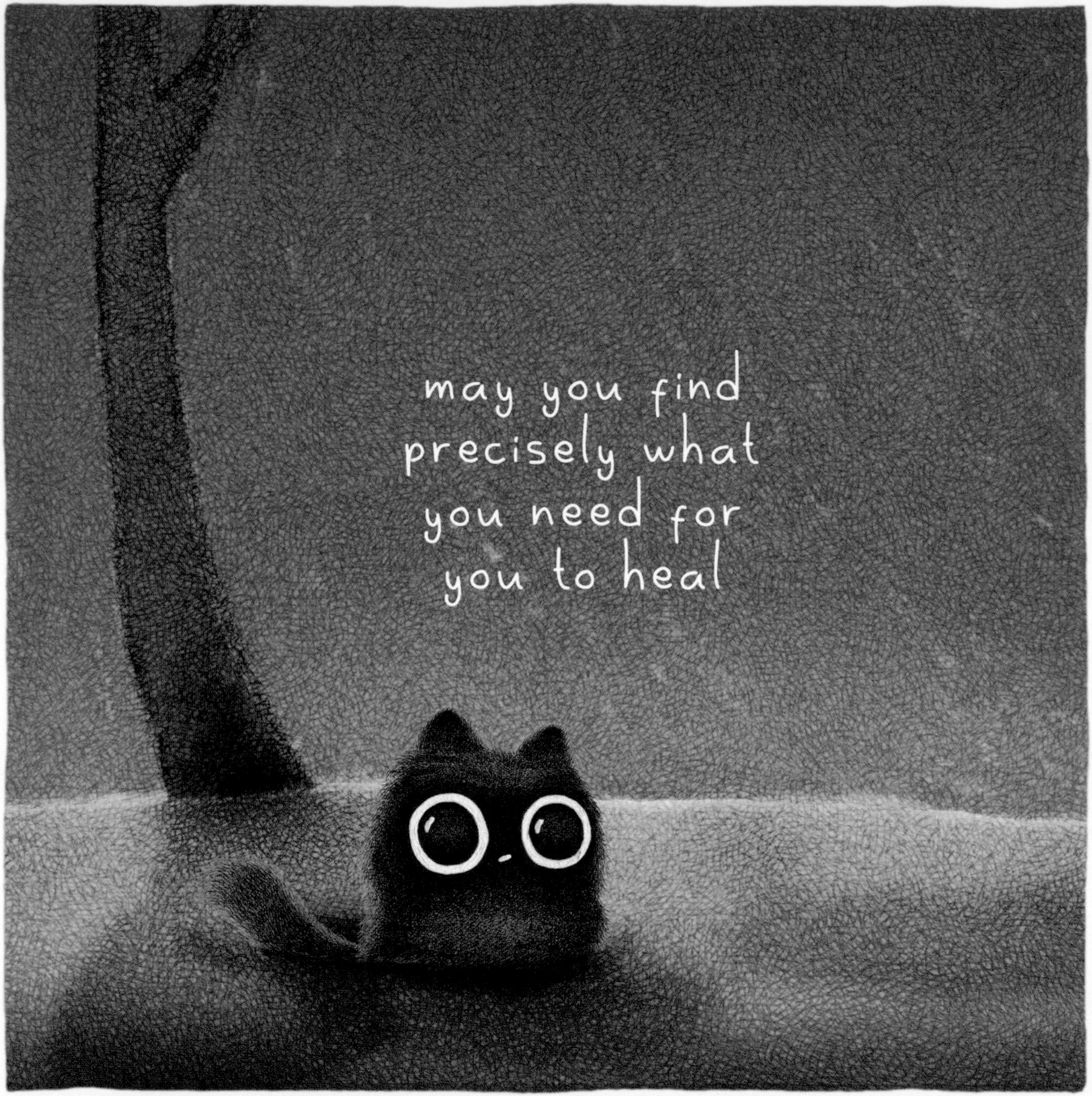
may you find
precisely what
you need for
you to heal

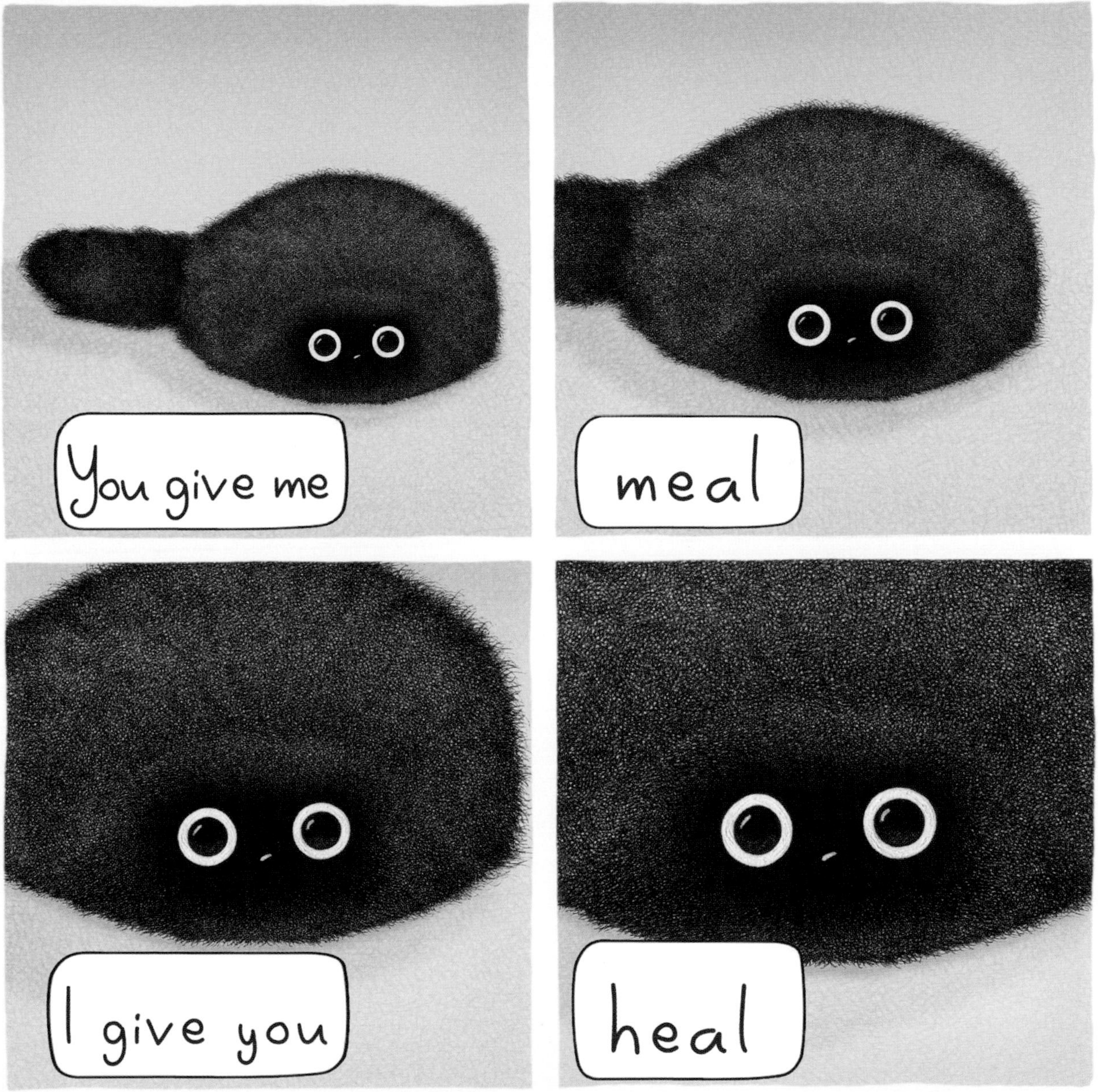
You give me
meal
I give you
heal

I just wanted
to remind you
that you are truly
an amazing being
with so much to
offer the world

Thinking about how much I love you

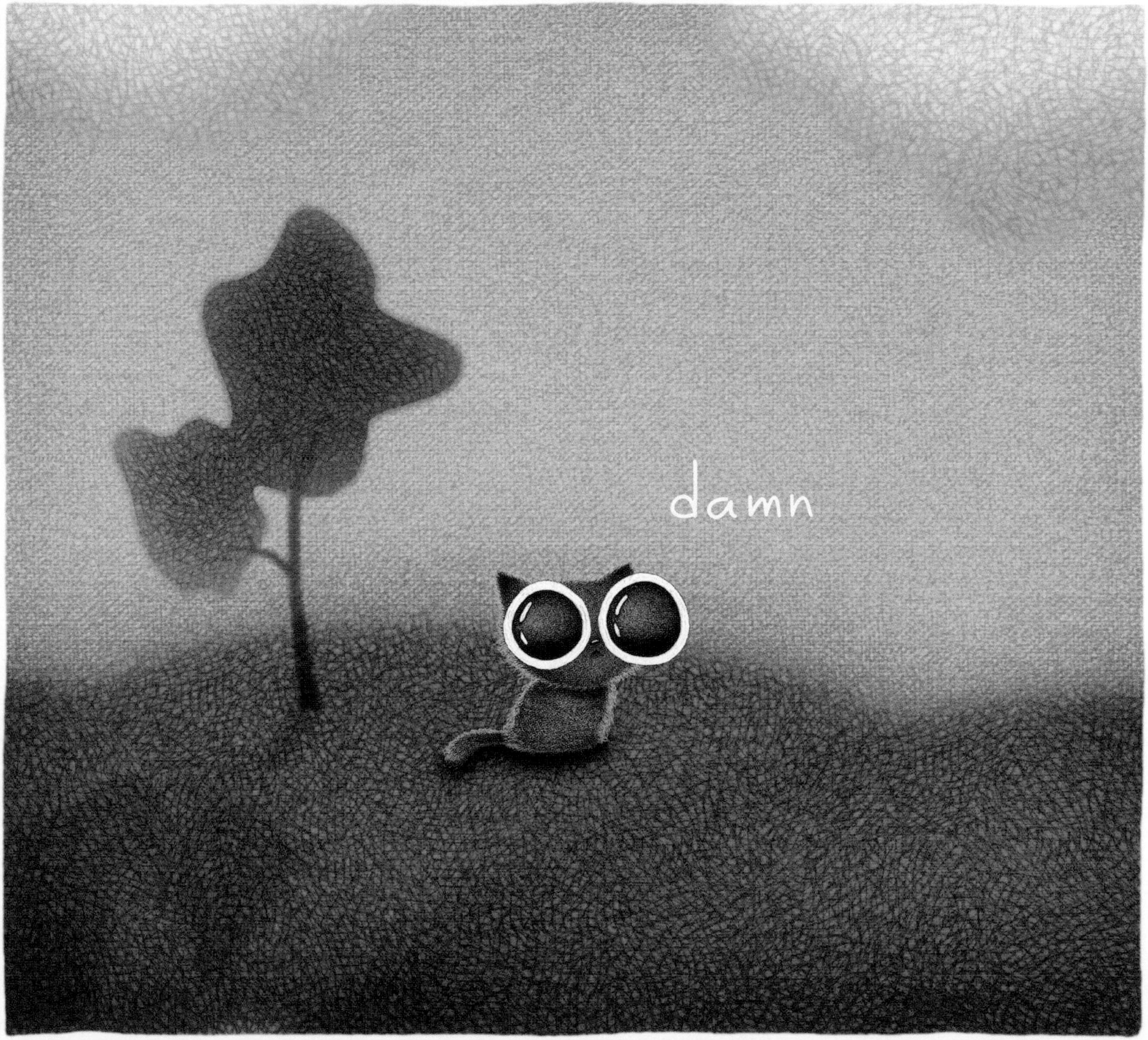
damn

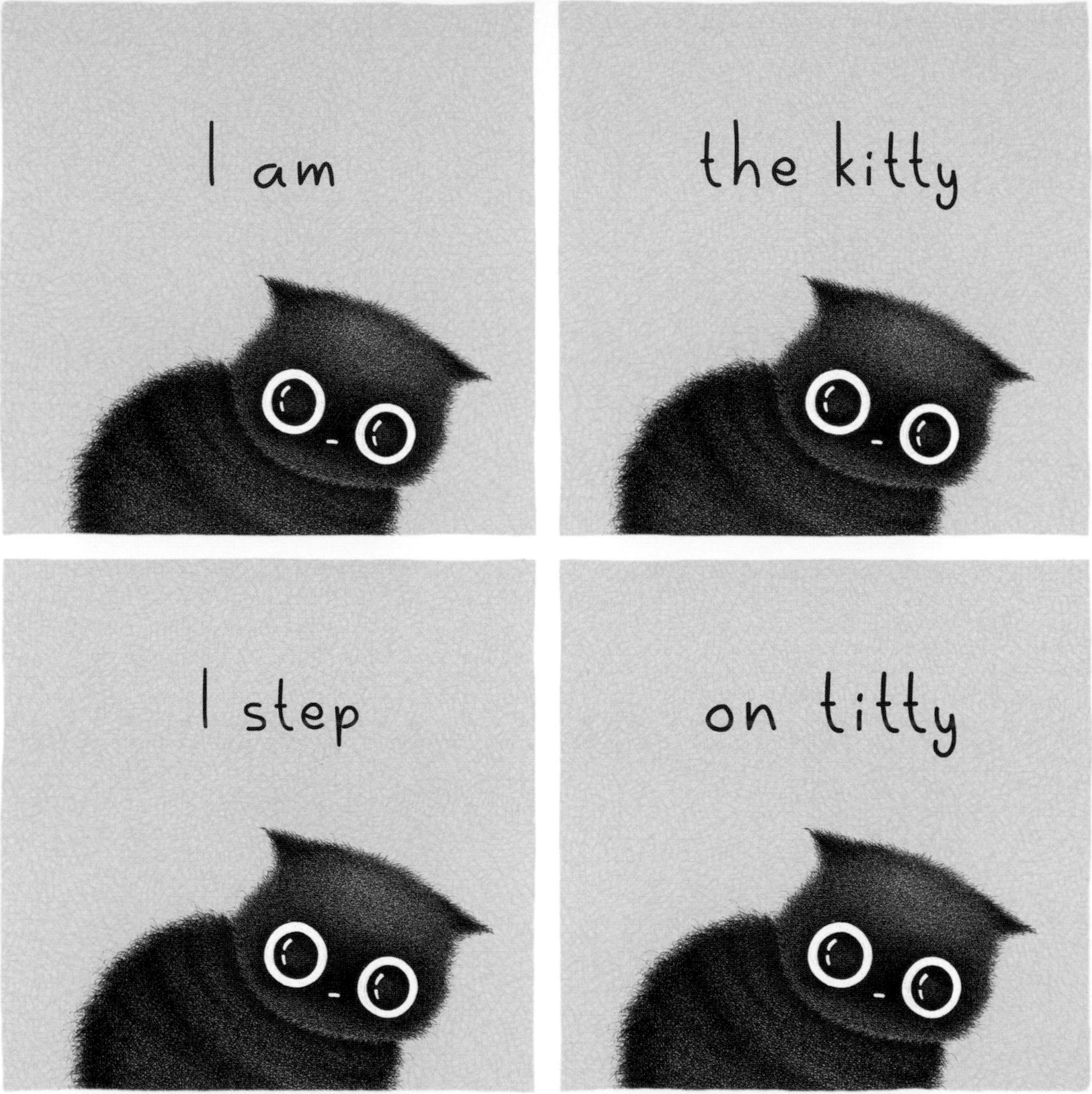
I am
the kitty
I step
on titty

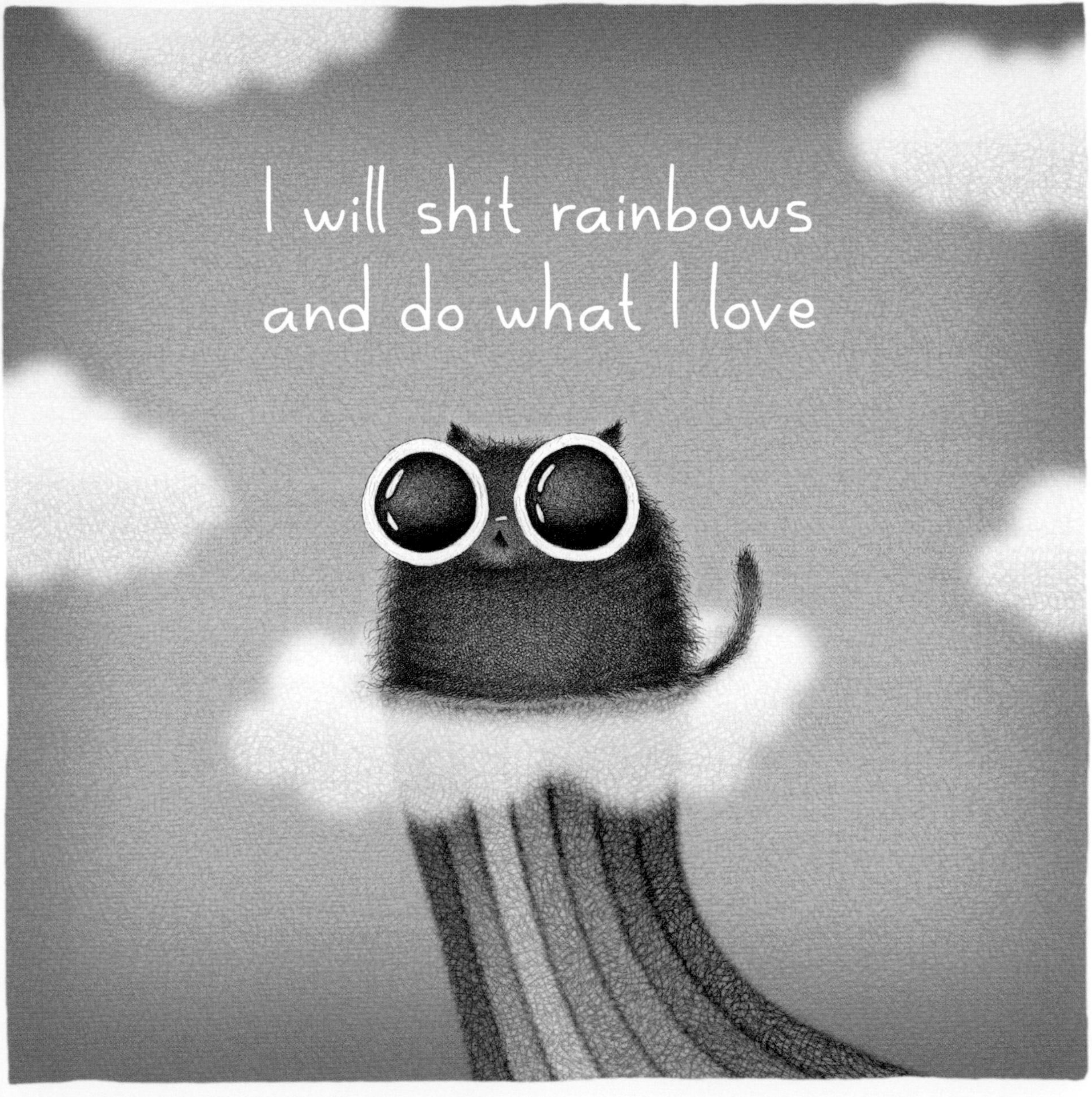
I will shit rainbows
and do what I love

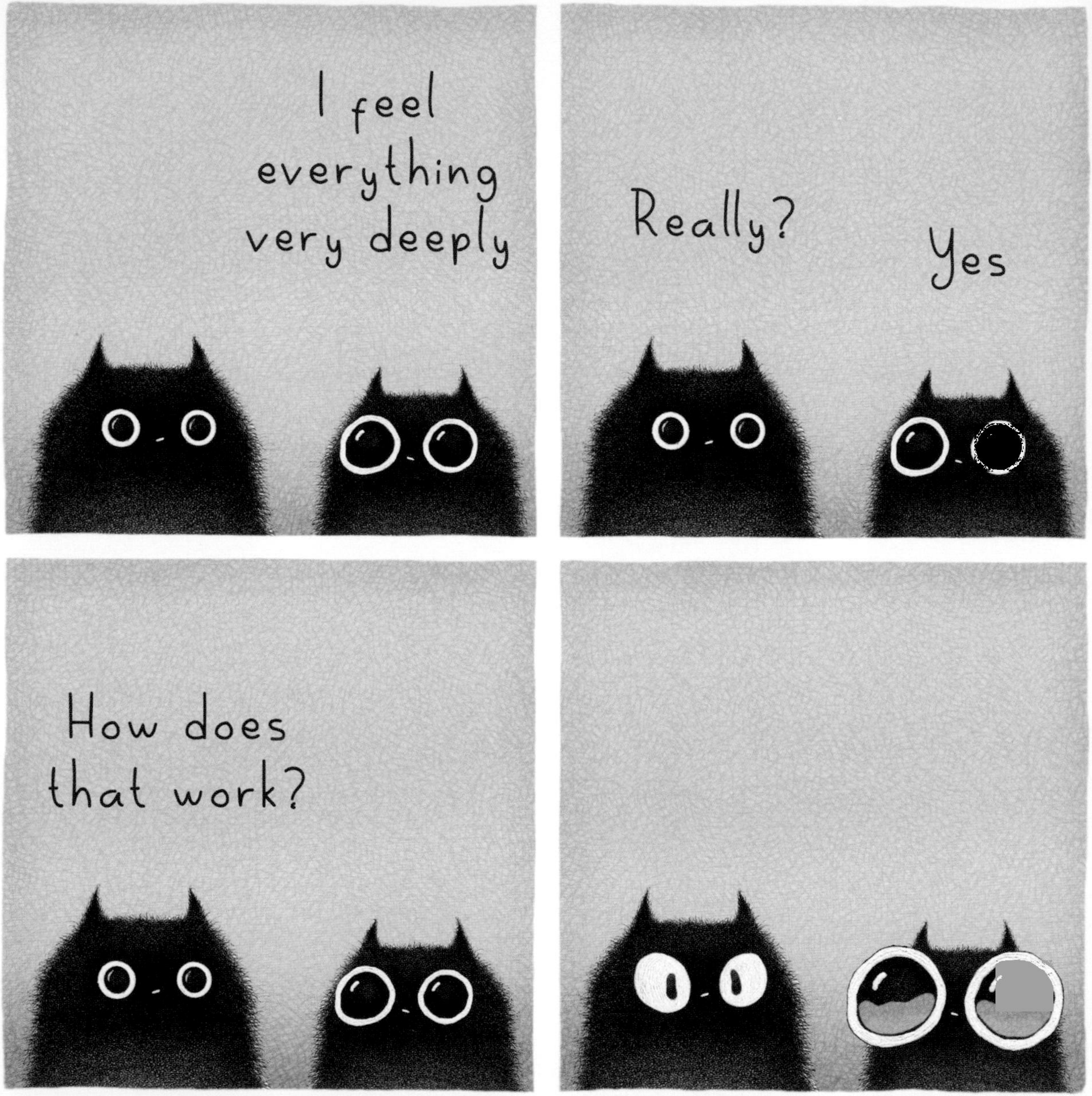
I feel everything very deeply
Really?
Yes
How does that work?

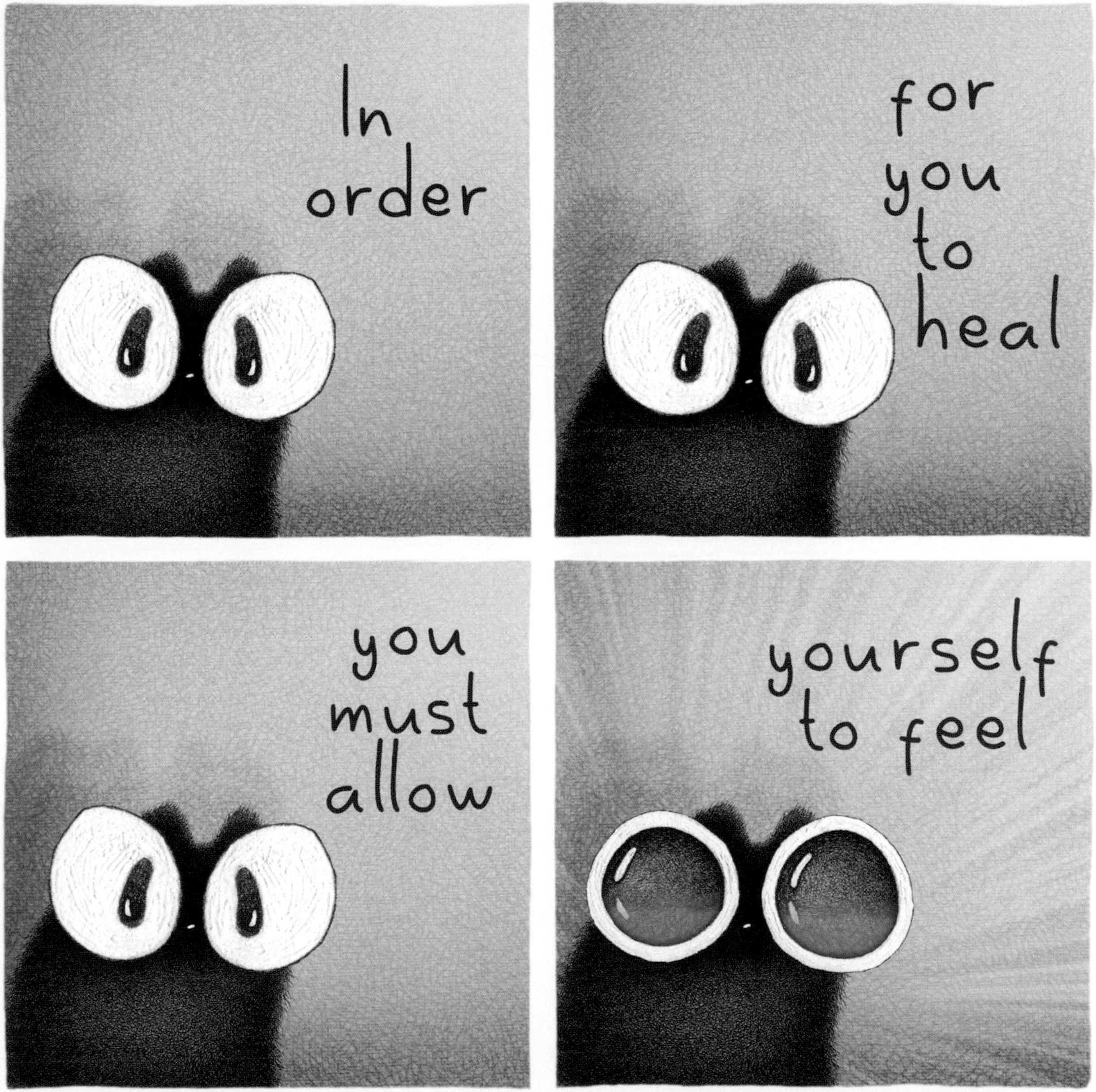
In order
for you to heal
you must allow
yourself to feel

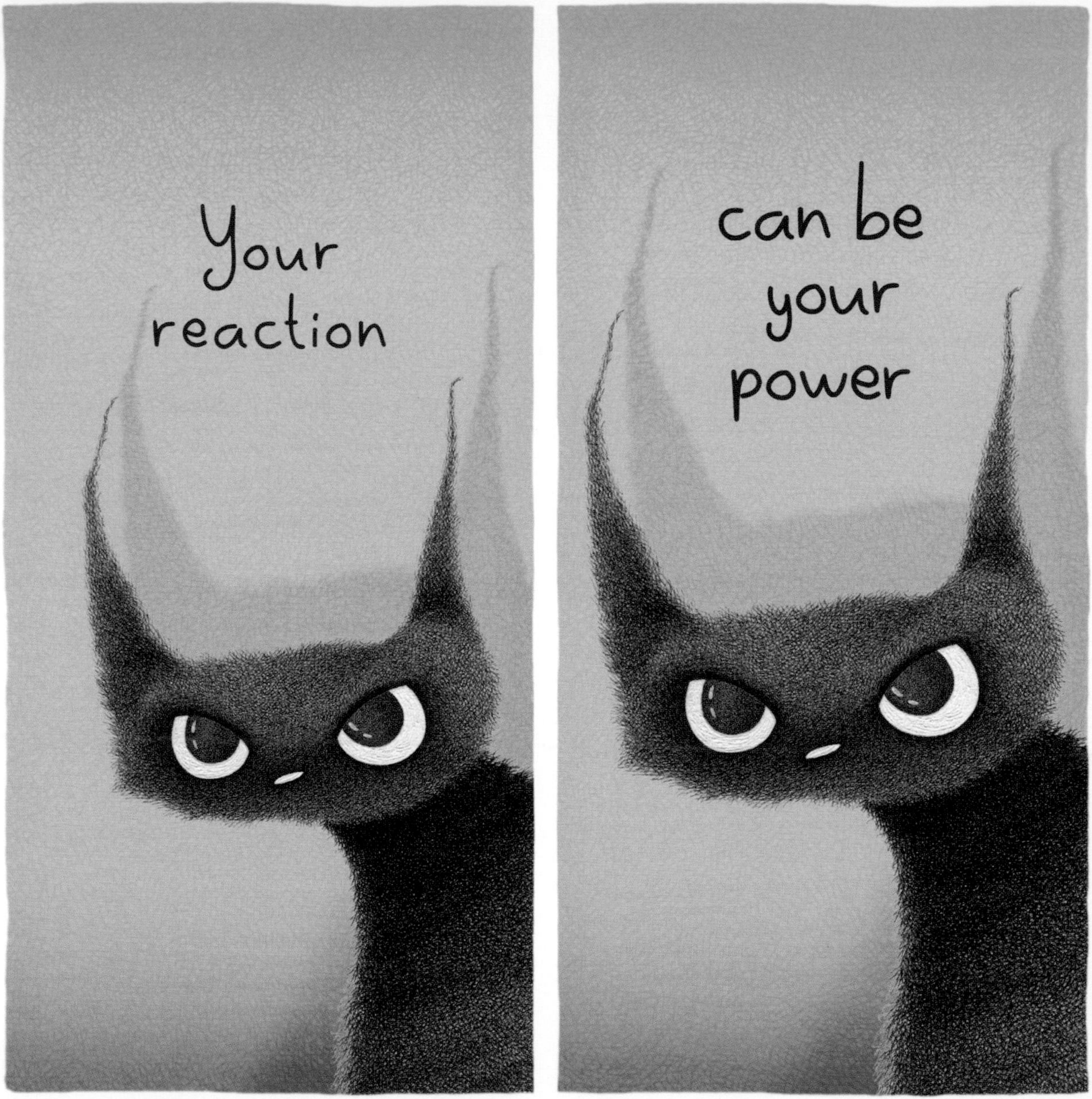
Your reaction
can be your power

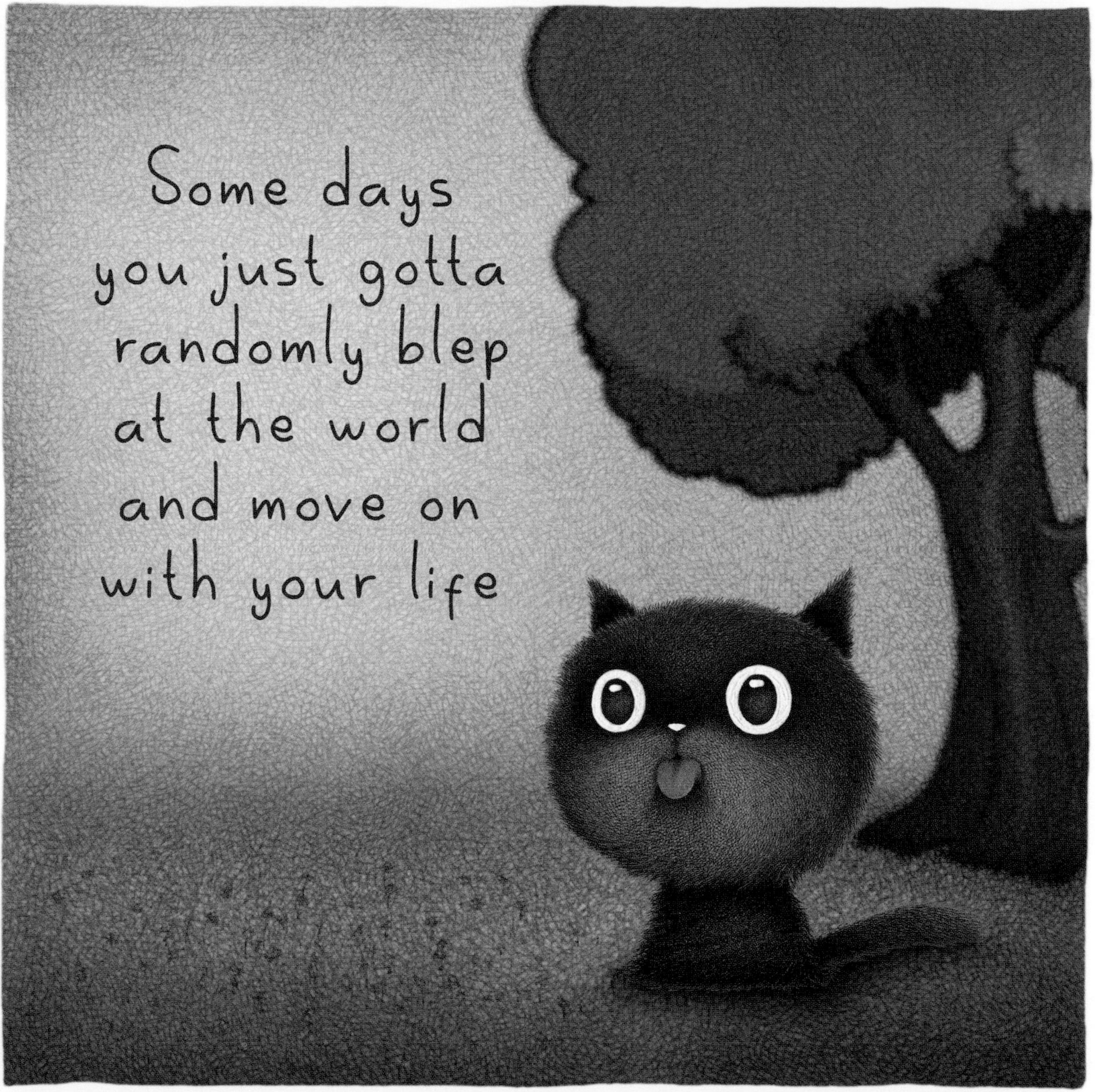
Some days
you just gotta
randomly blep
at the world
and move on
with your life

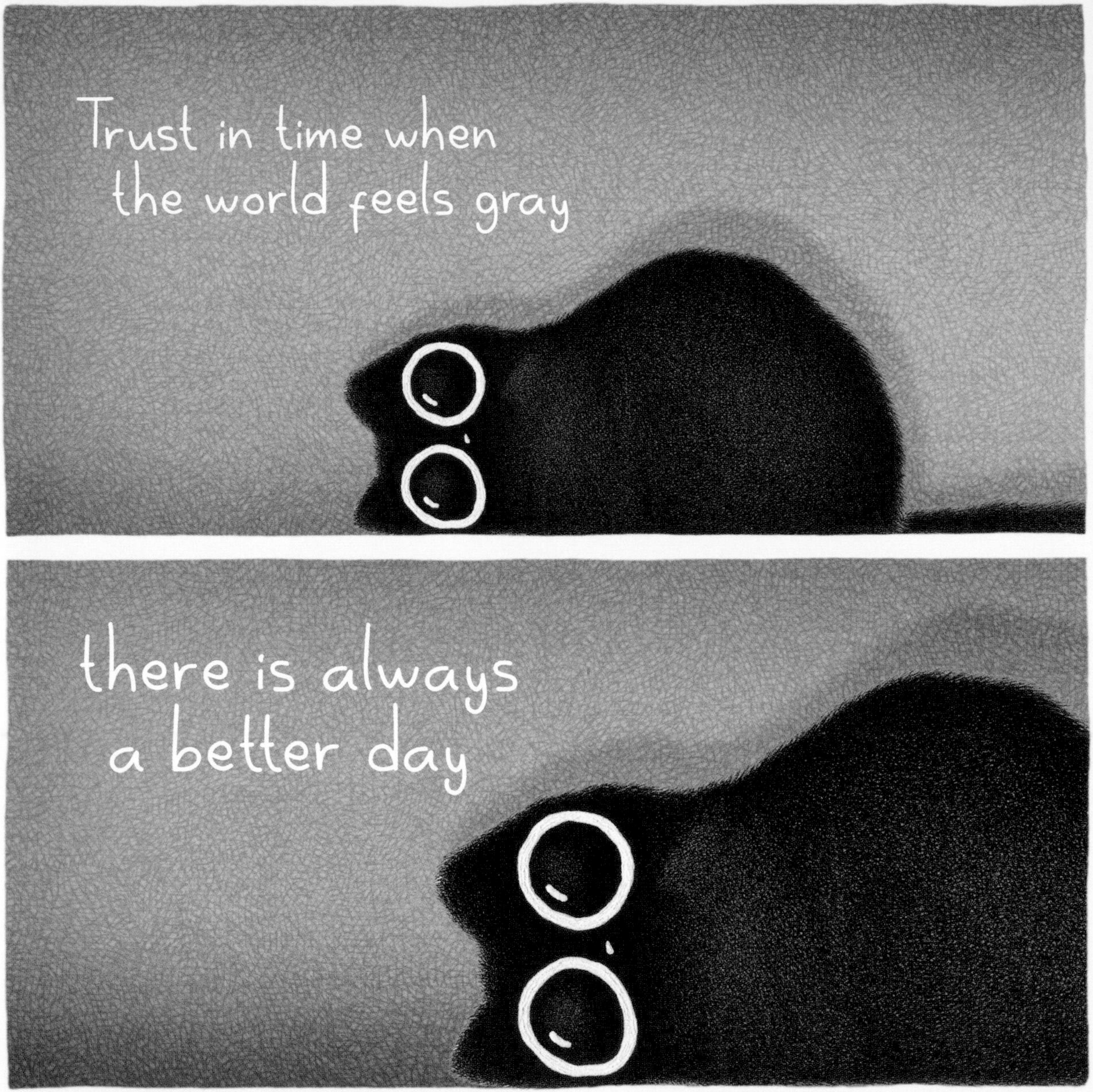
Trust in time when
the world feels gray
there is always
a better day

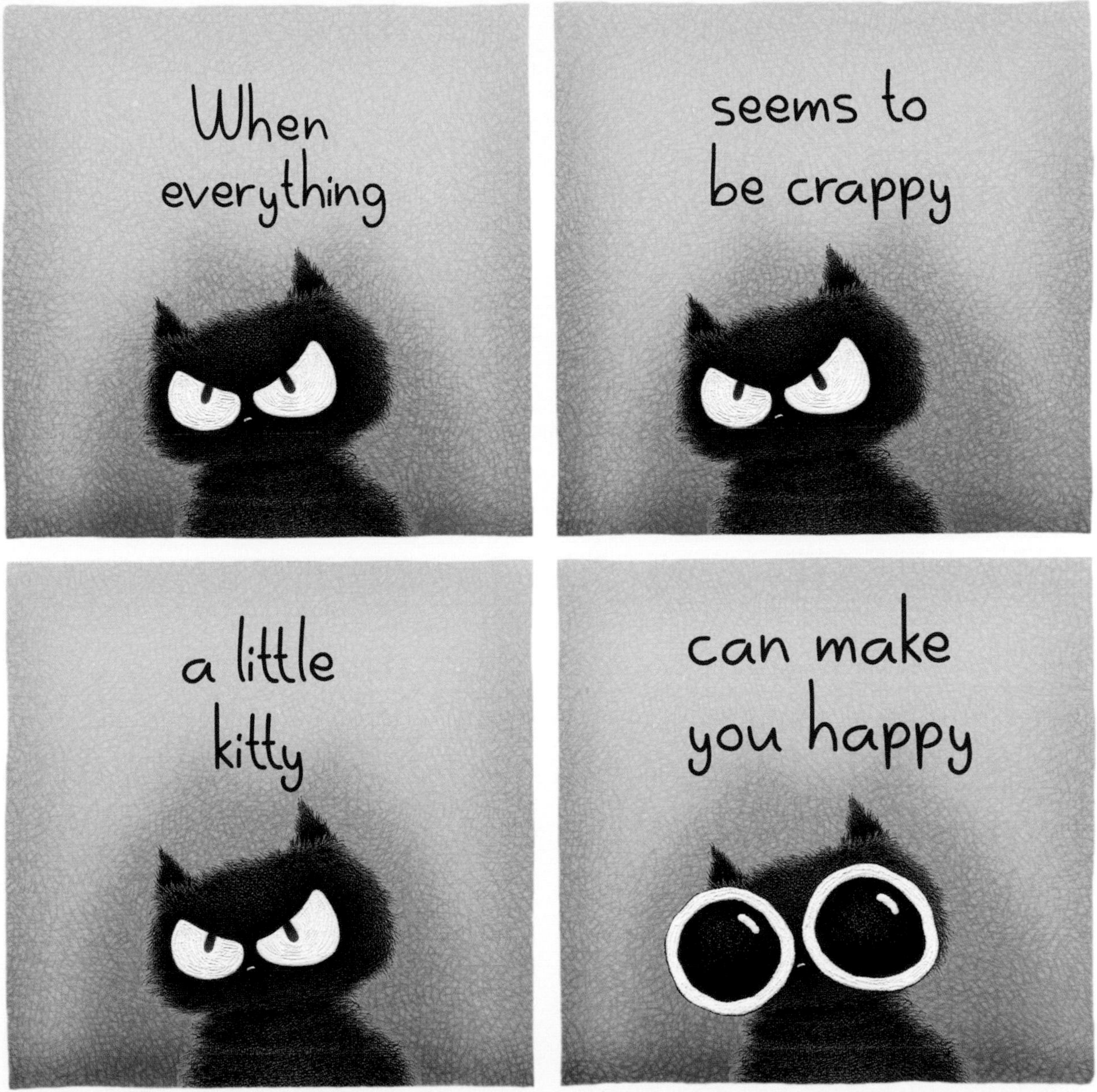
When everything
seems to be crappy
a little kitty
can make you happy

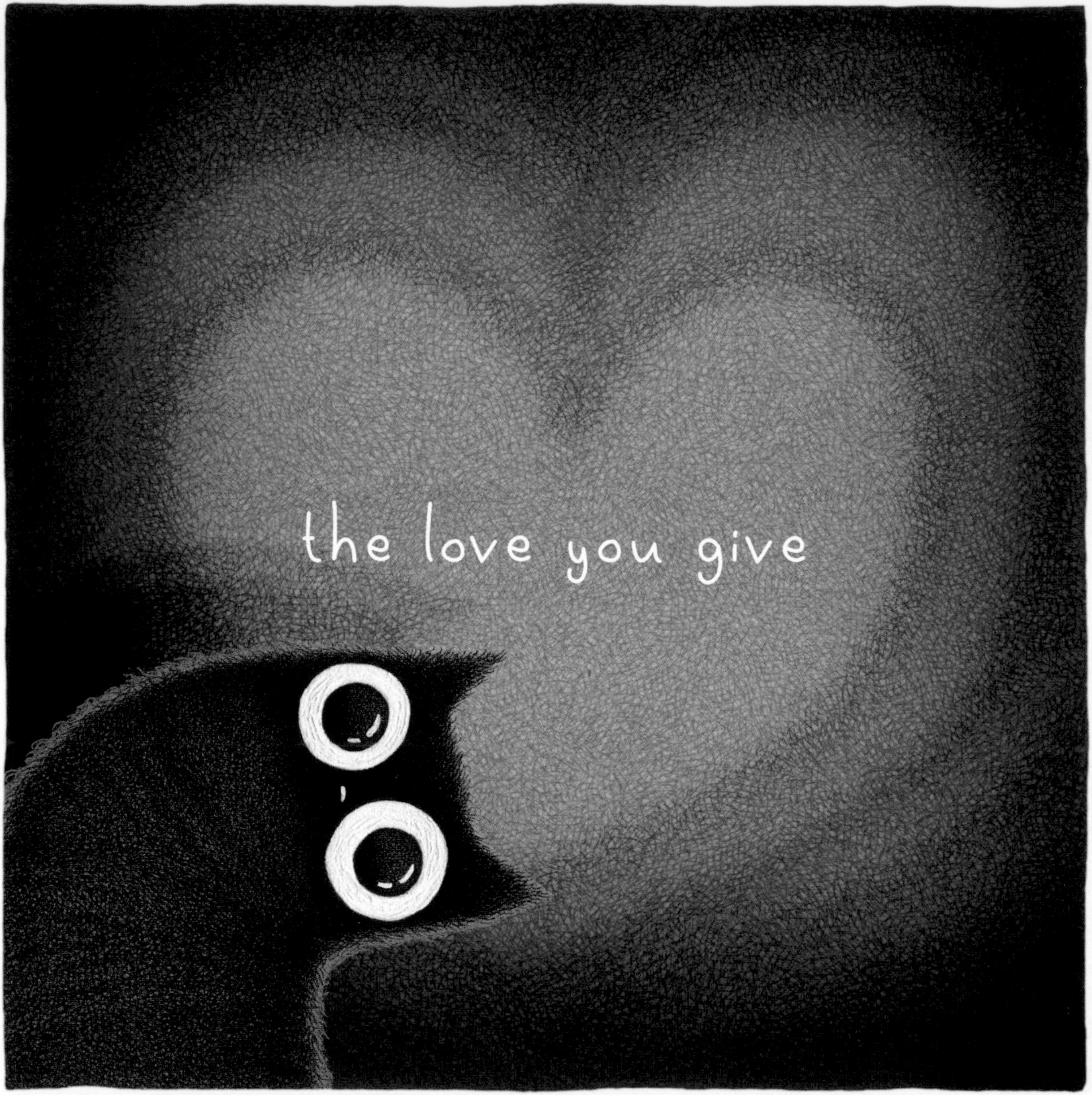
the love you give

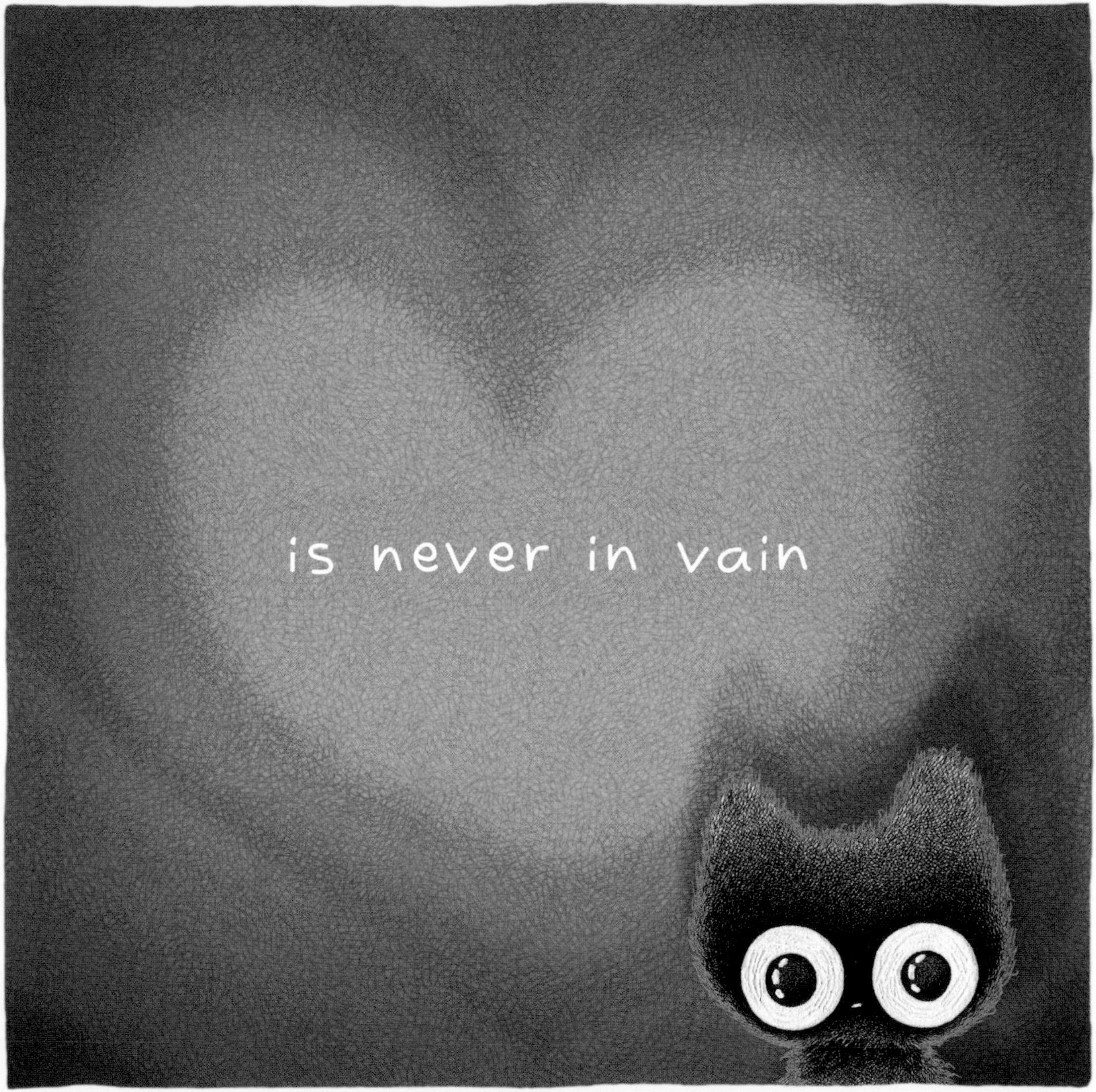
is never in vain

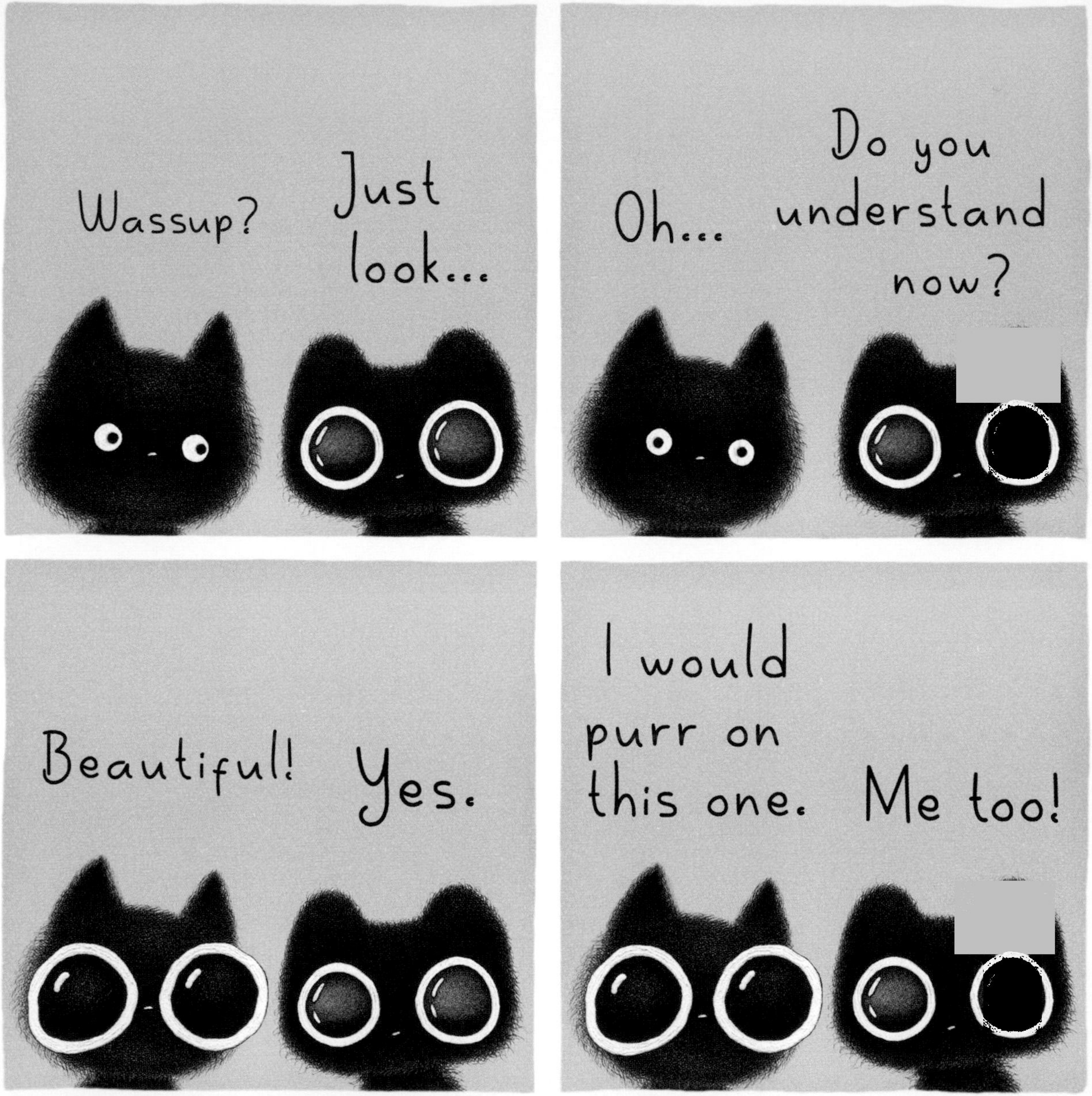
Wassup?
Just look...
Oh...
Do you understand now?
Beautiful!
Yes.
I would purr on this one.
Me too!

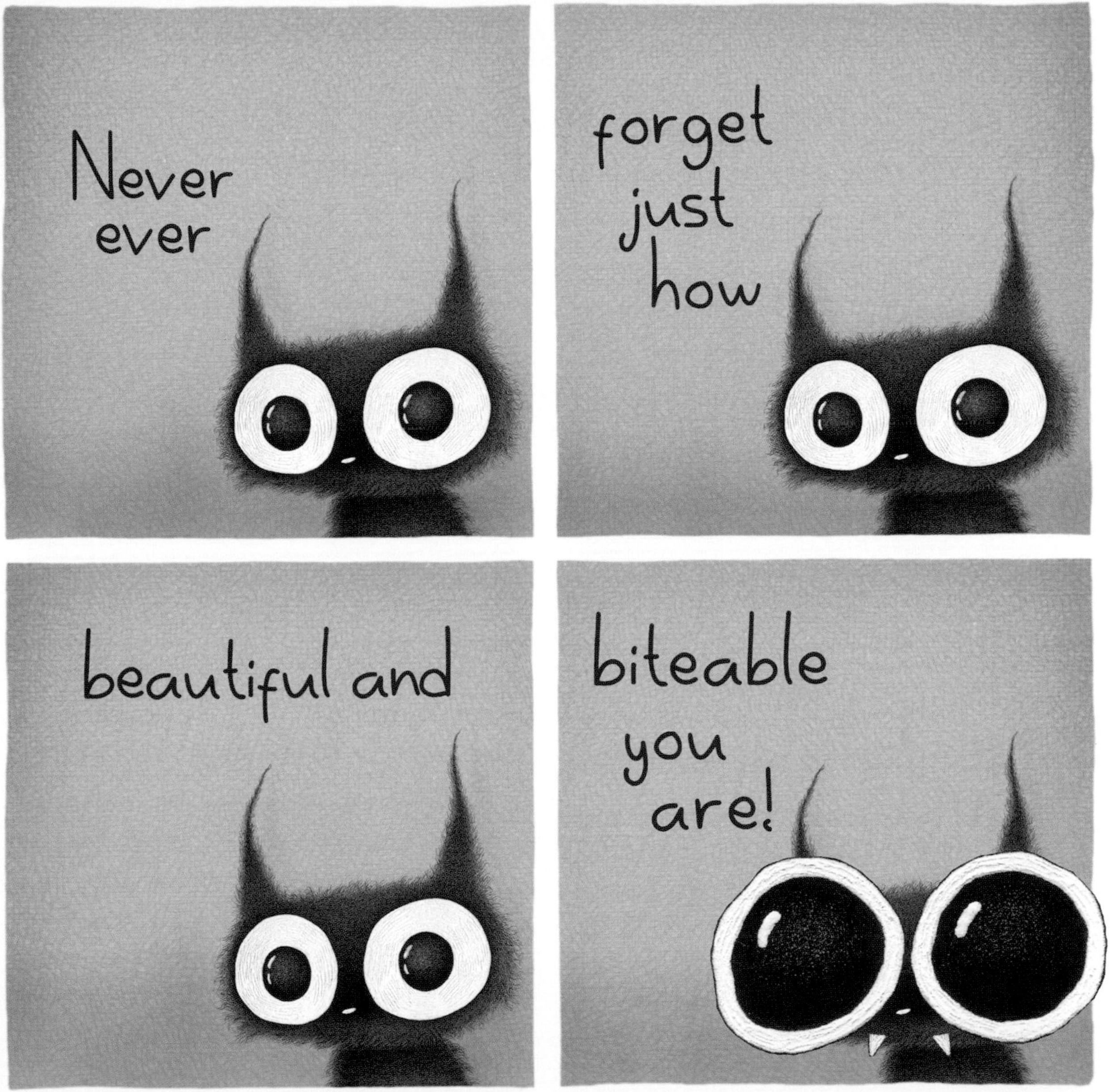
Never
ever
forget
just
how
beautiful and
biteable
you
are!

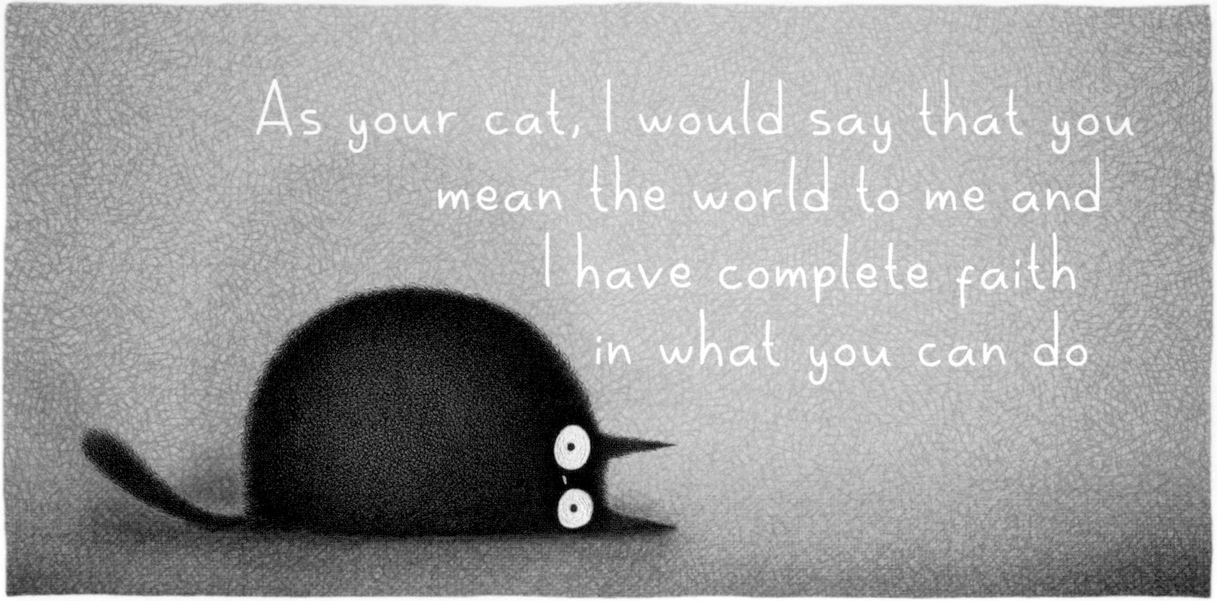
As your cat, I would say that you mean the world to me and I have complete faith in what you can do

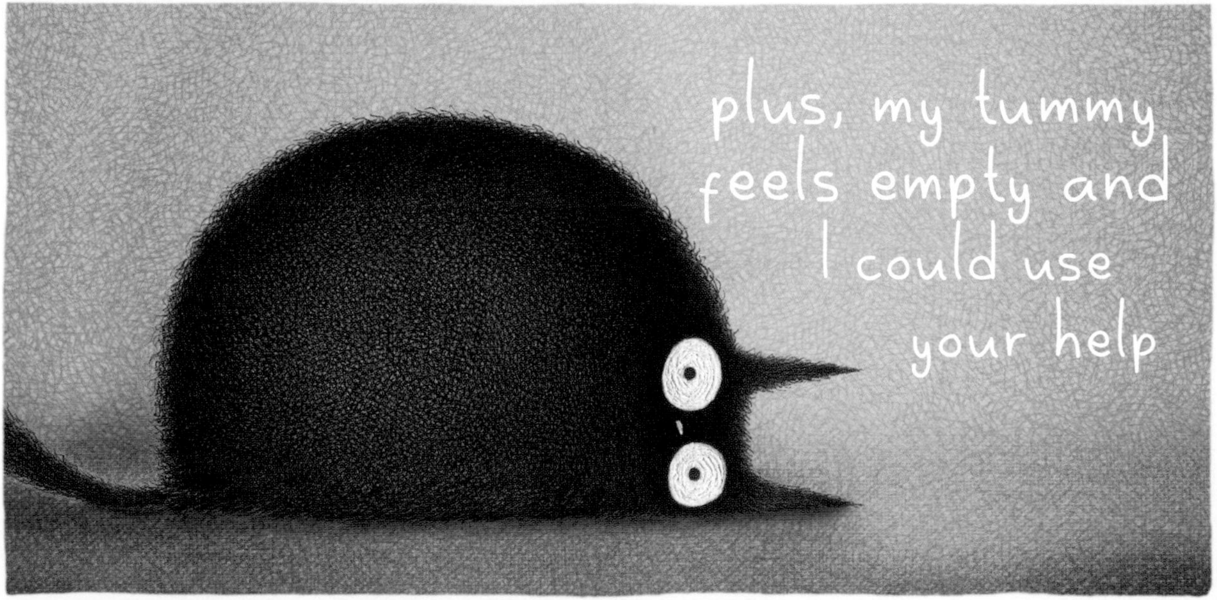
plus, my tummy feels empty and I could use your help

Have you ever heard that
spreading love and kindness
will also make you happier?

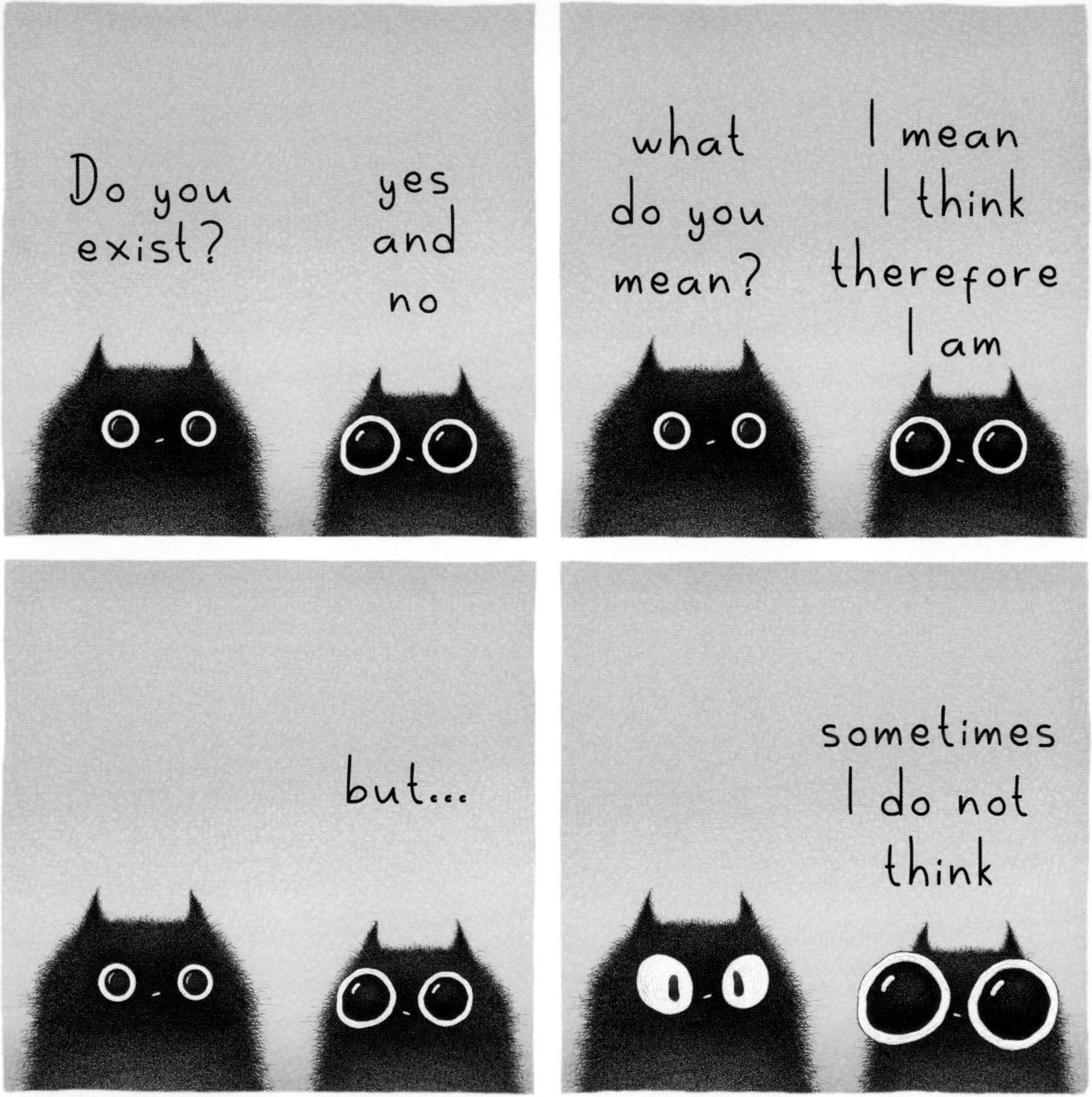
Do you exist?
yes and no
what do you mean?
I mean I think therefore I am
but...
sometimes I do not think

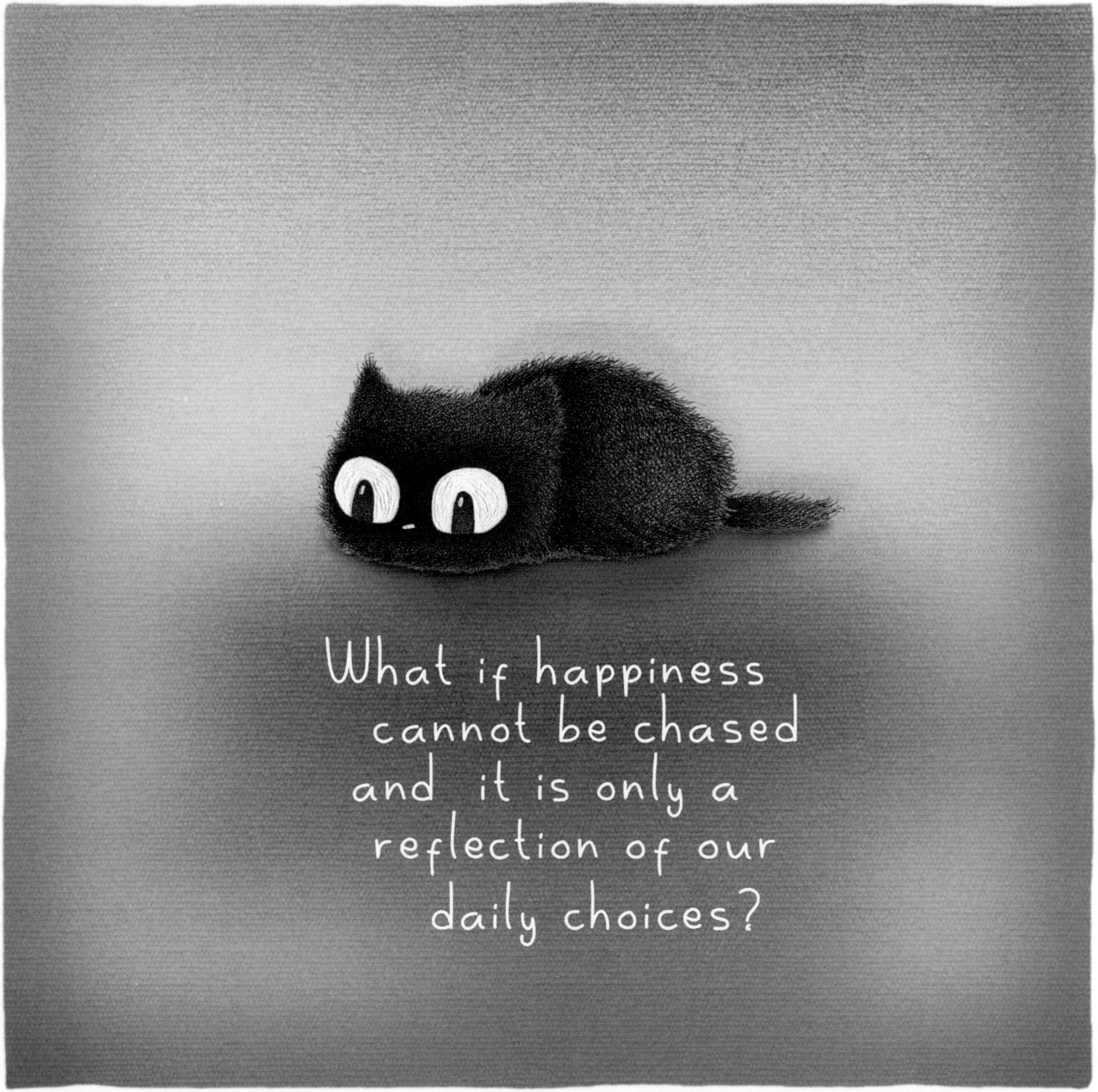
What if happiness
cannot be chased
and it is only a
reflection of our
daily choices?

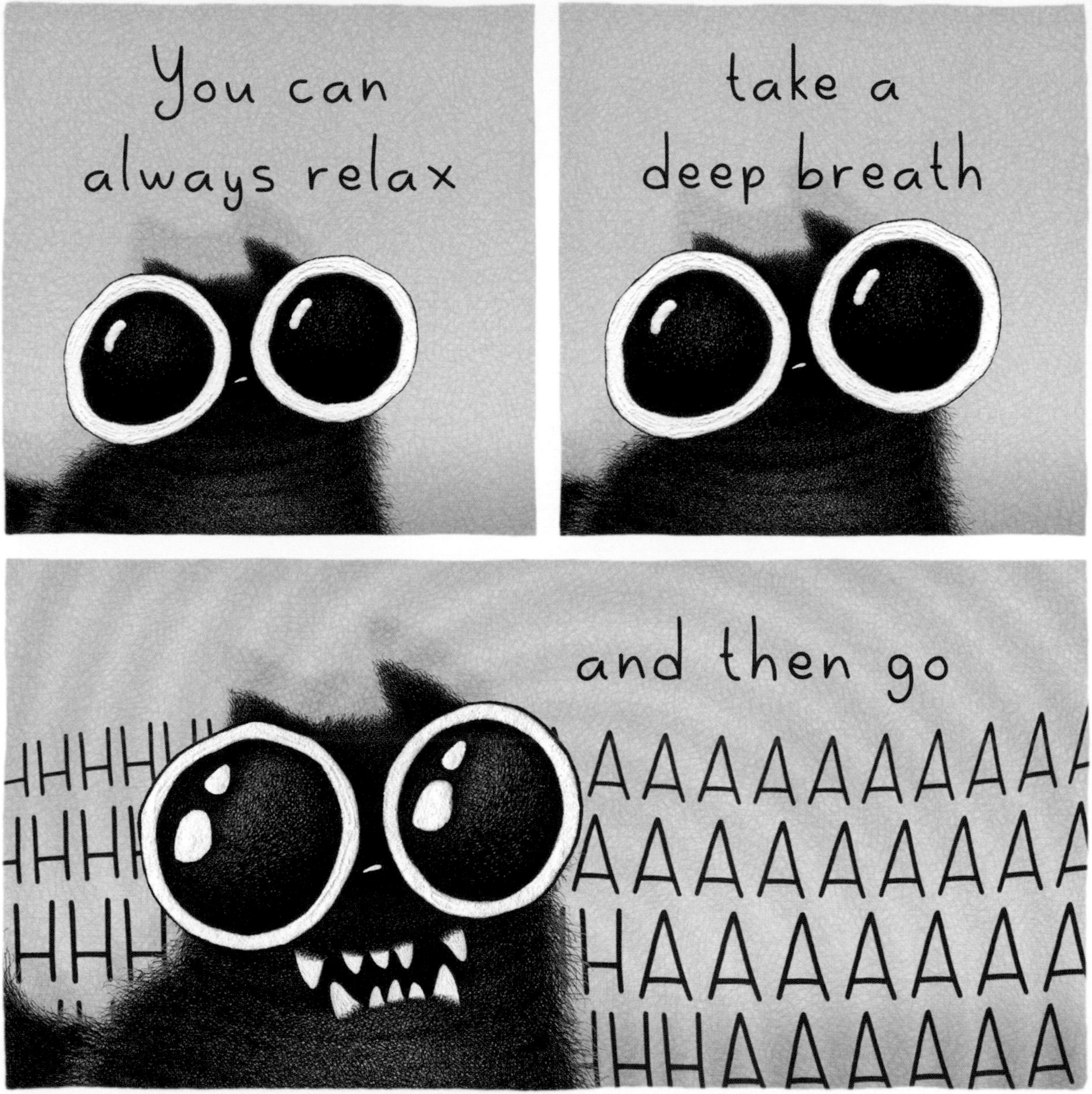
You can always relax
take a deep breath
and then go
HHHH
HHHH
HHH
AAAAAAAAA
AAAAAAAAA
HAAAAAAAA
HHAAAAAAA

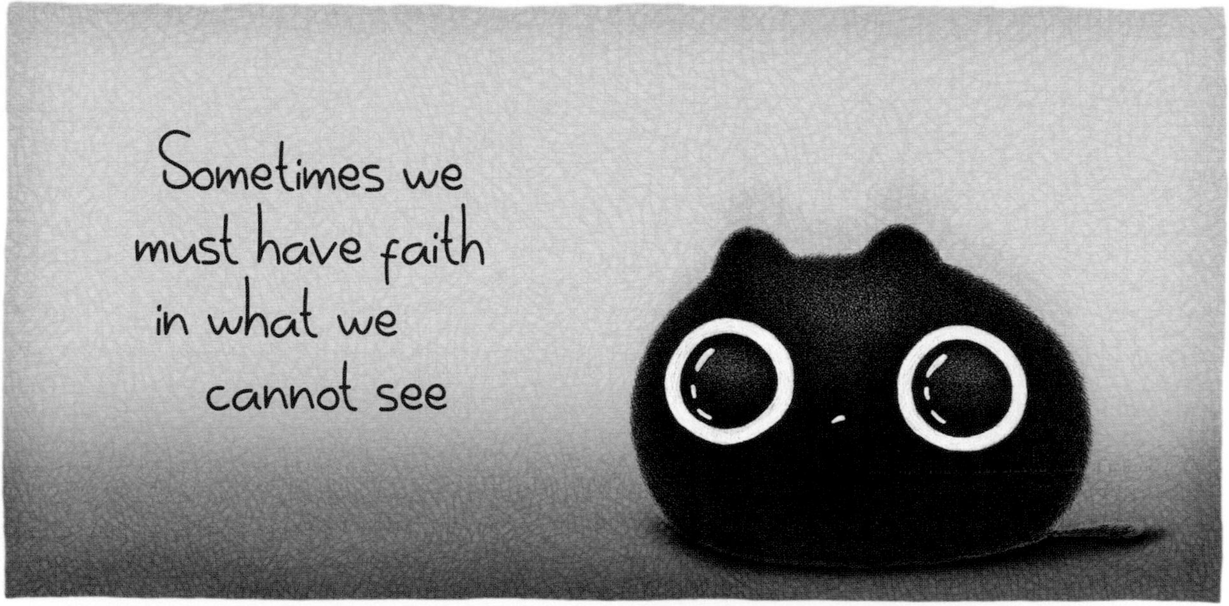
Sometimes we
must have faith
in what we
cannot see

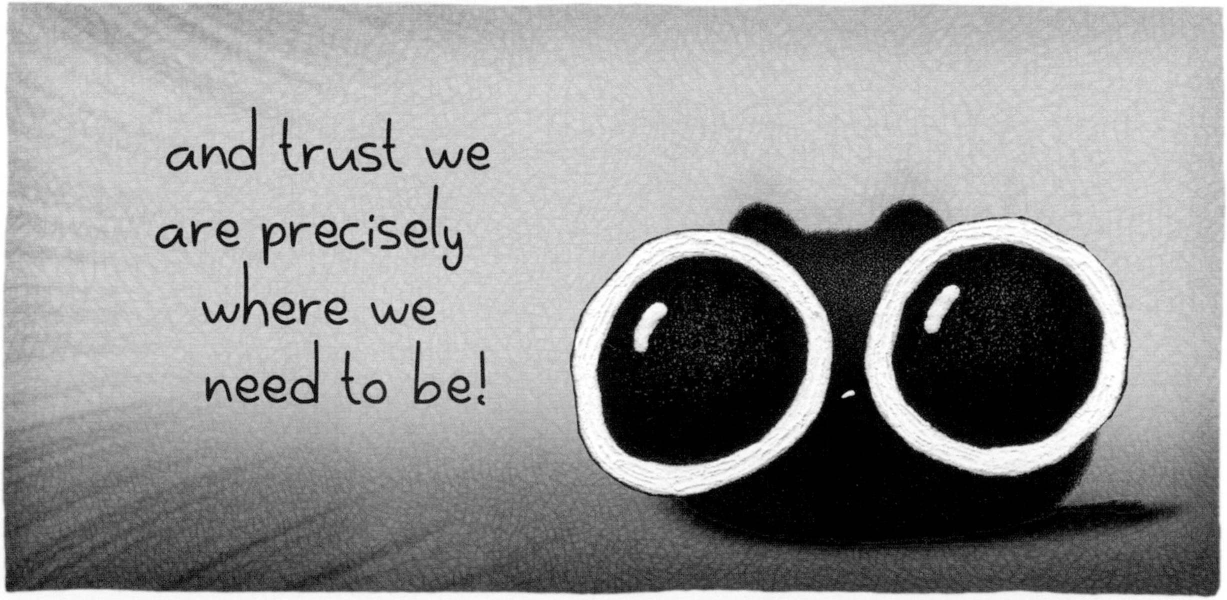
and trust we
are precisely
where we
need to be!

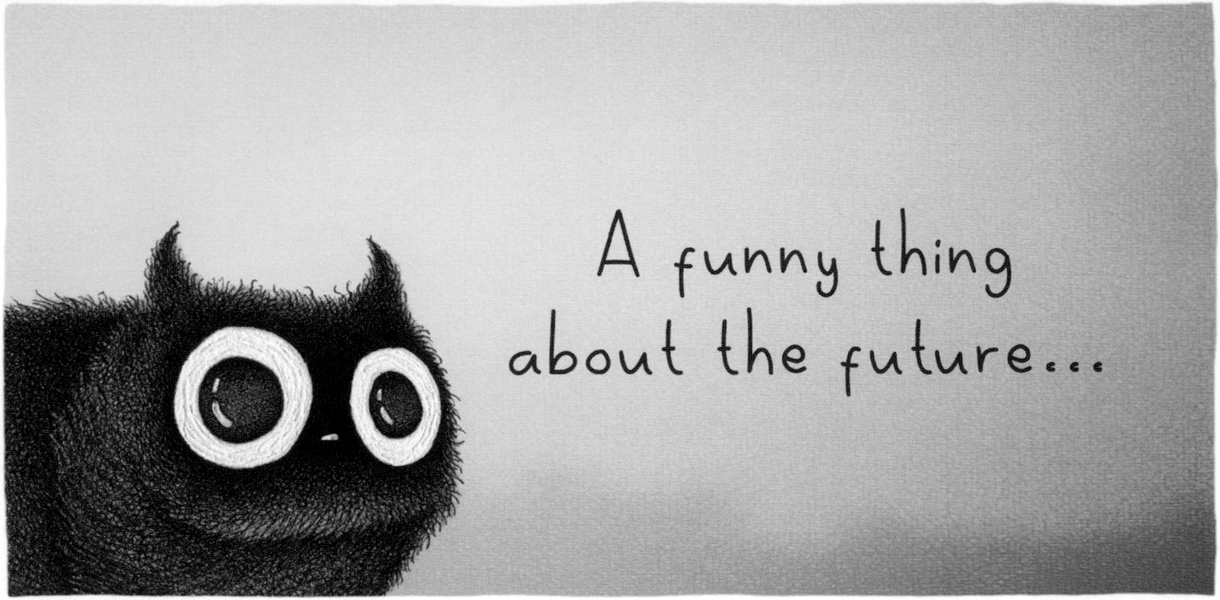
A funny thing
about the future...

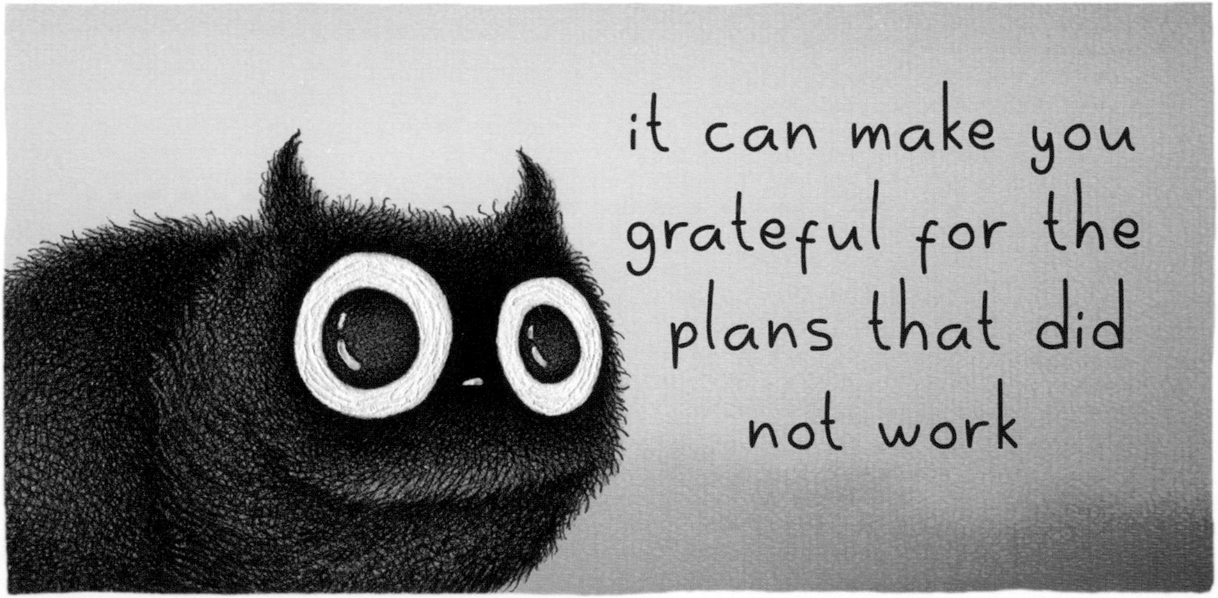
it can make you
grateful for the
plans that did
not work

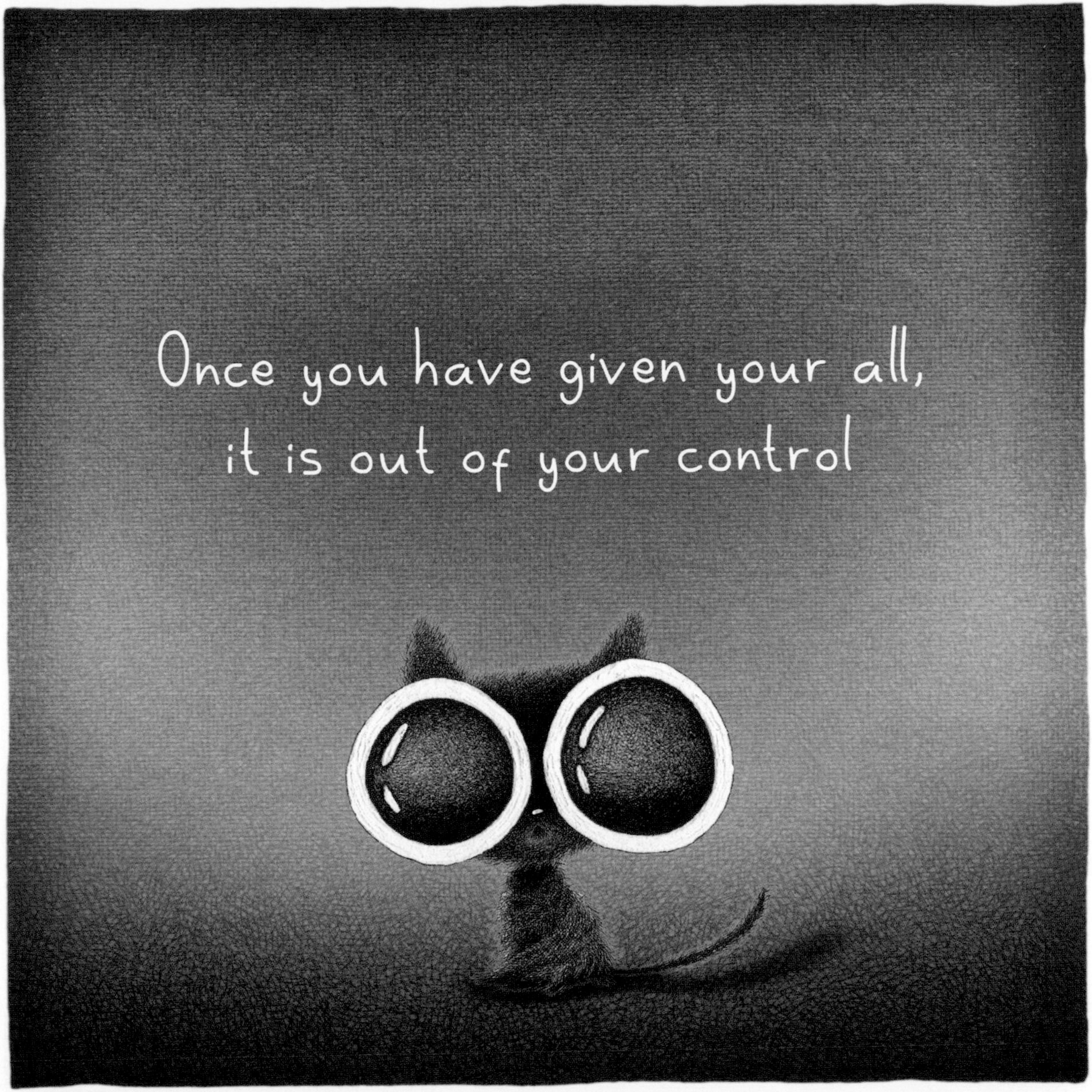
Once you have given your all,
it is out of your control

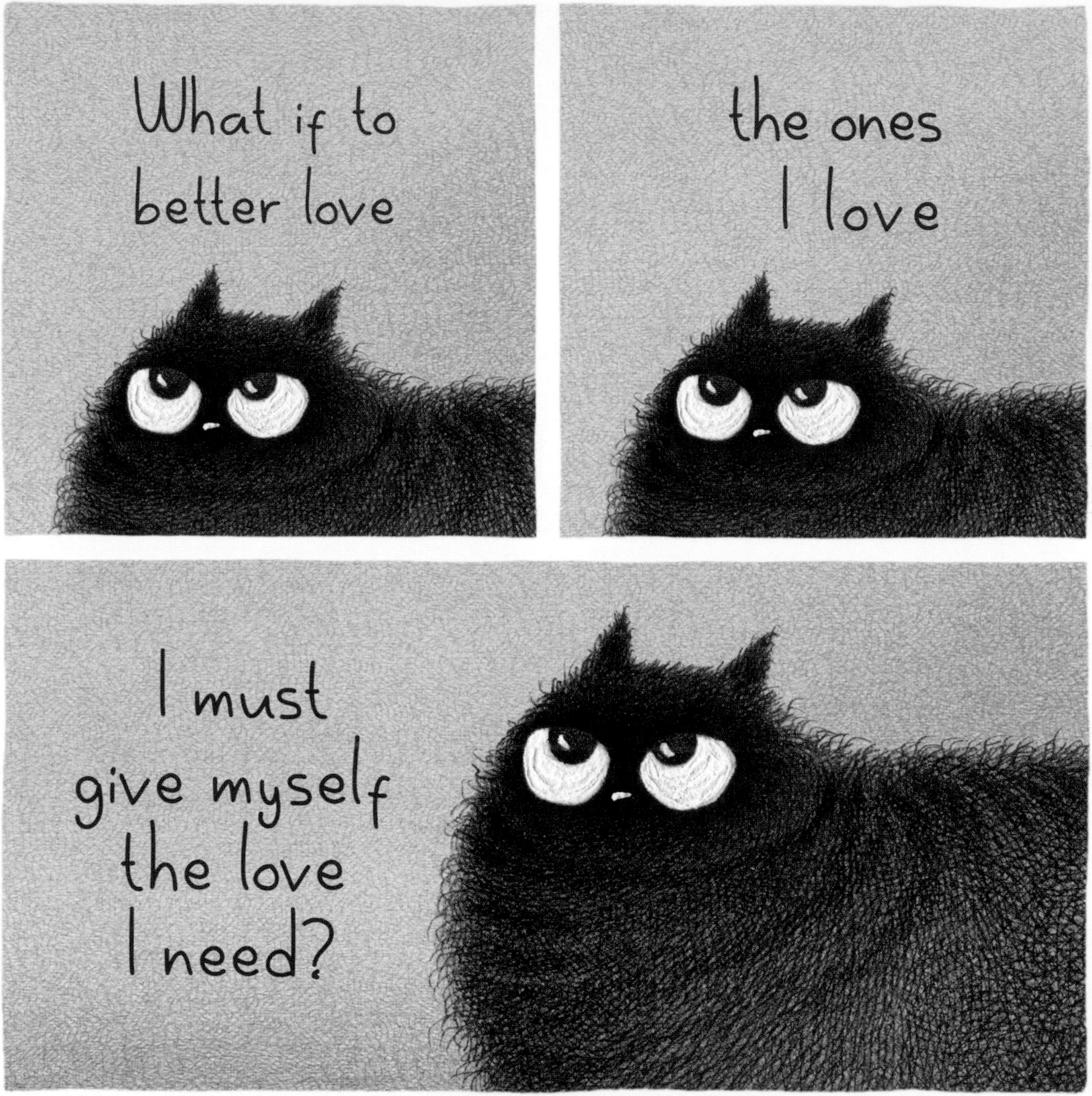
What if to better love
the ones I love
I must give myself the love I need?

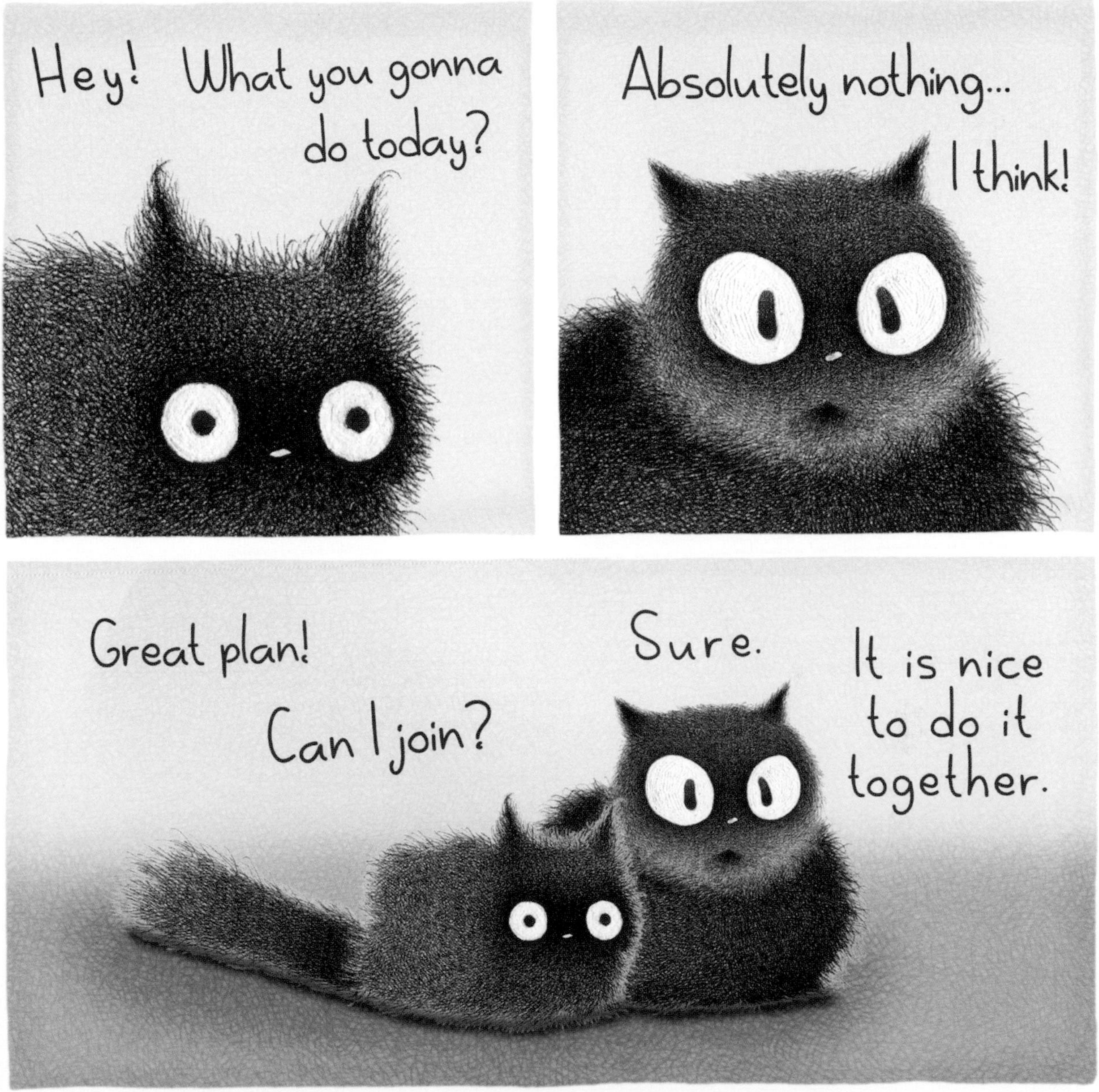
Hey! What you gonna do today?
Absolutely nothing... I think!
Great plan!
Can I join?
Sure.
It is nice to do it together.

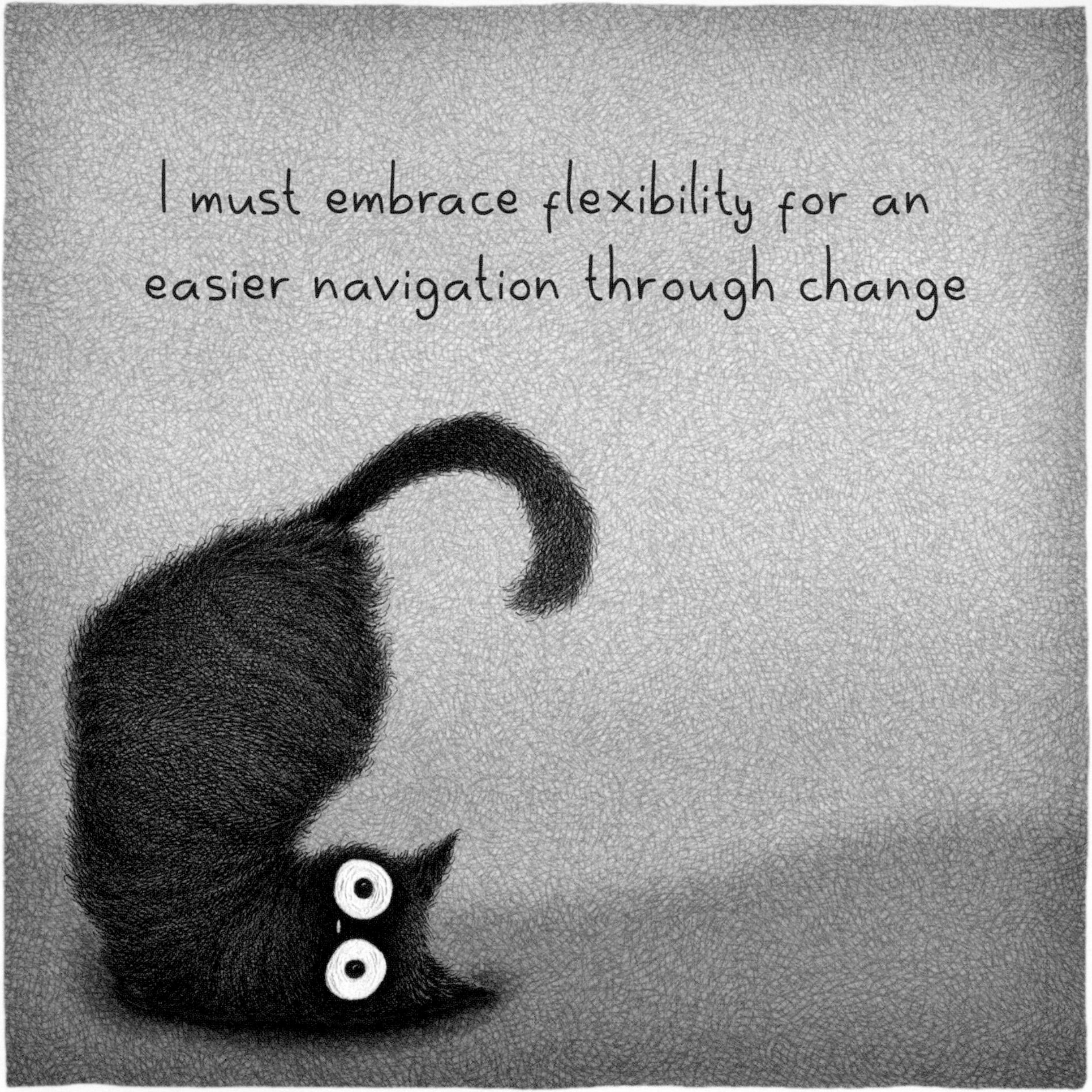
I must embrace flexibility for an
easier navigation through change

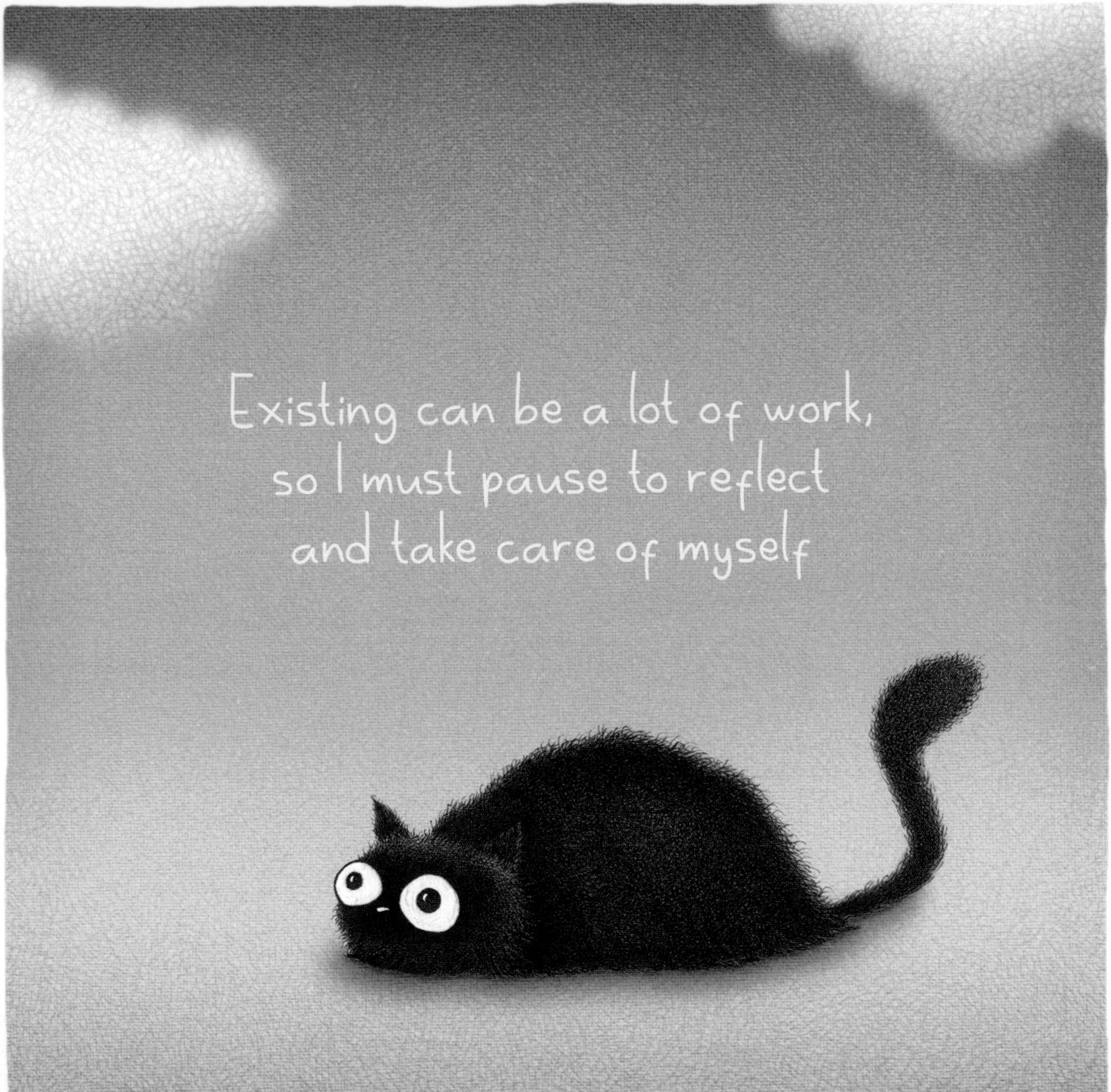
Existing can be a lot of work,
so I must pause to reflect
and take care of myself

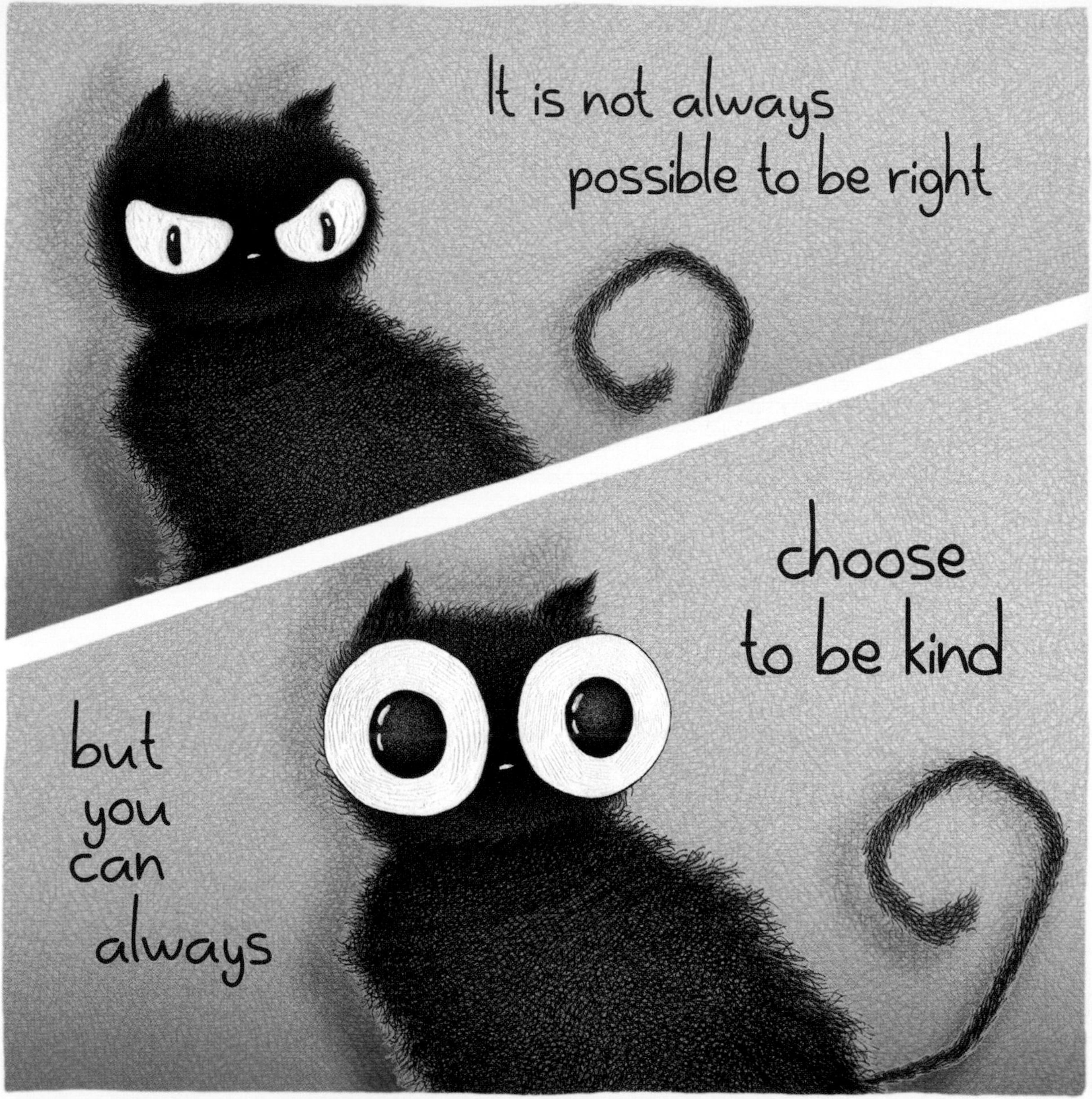
It is not always possible to be right
but you can always
choose to be kind

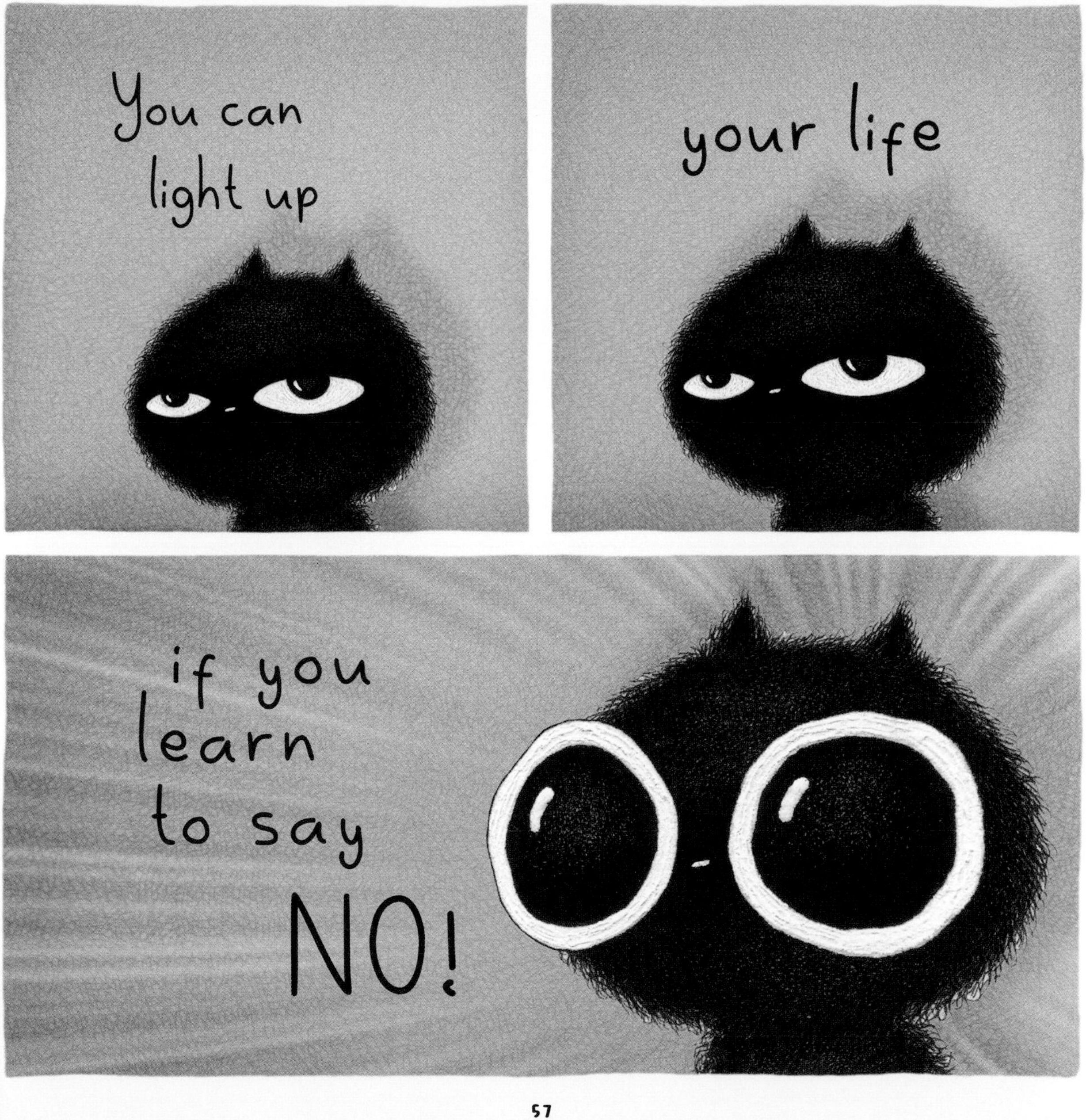
You can
light up
your life
if you
learn
to say
NO!

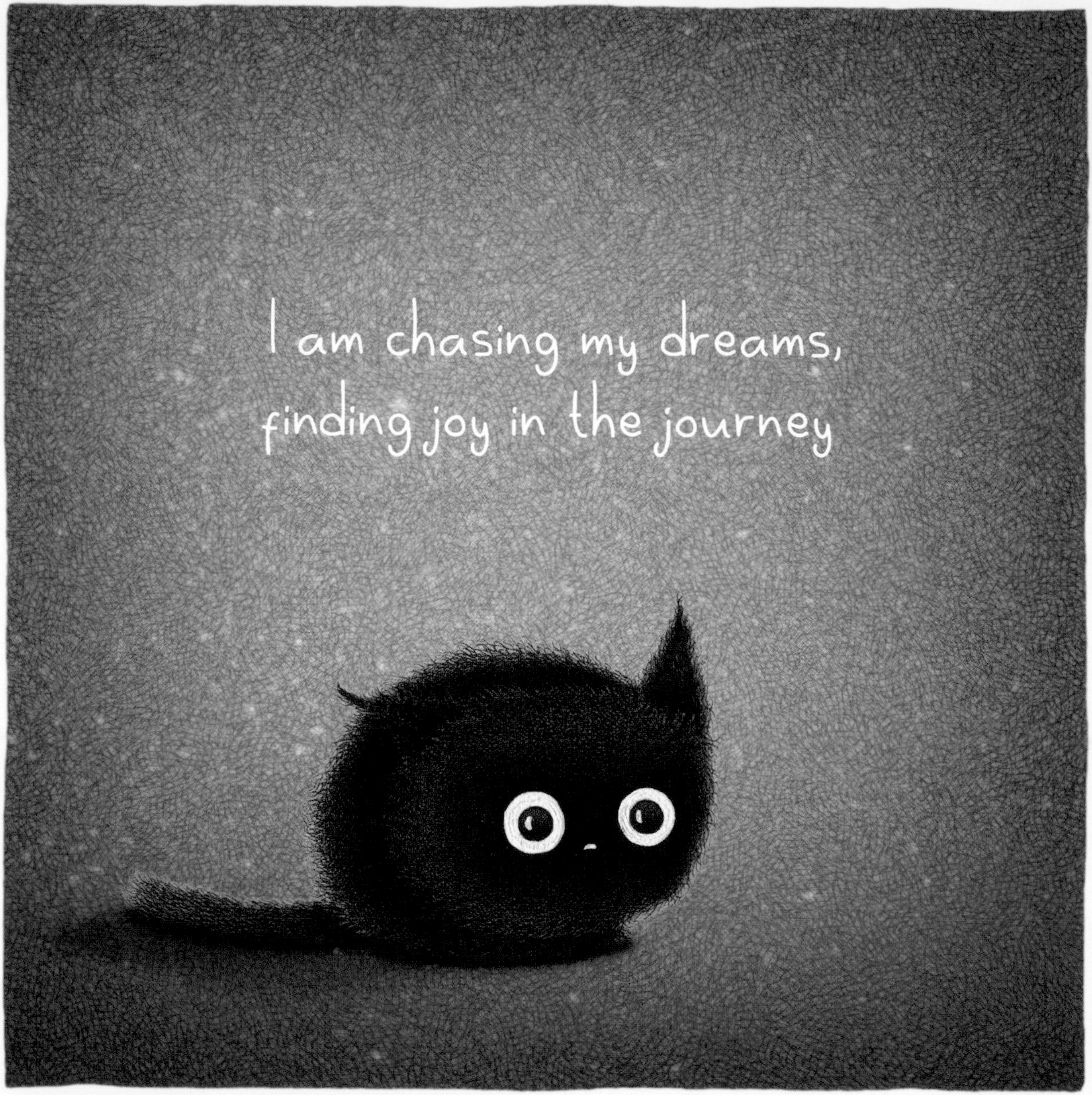
I am chasing my dreams,
finding joy in the journey

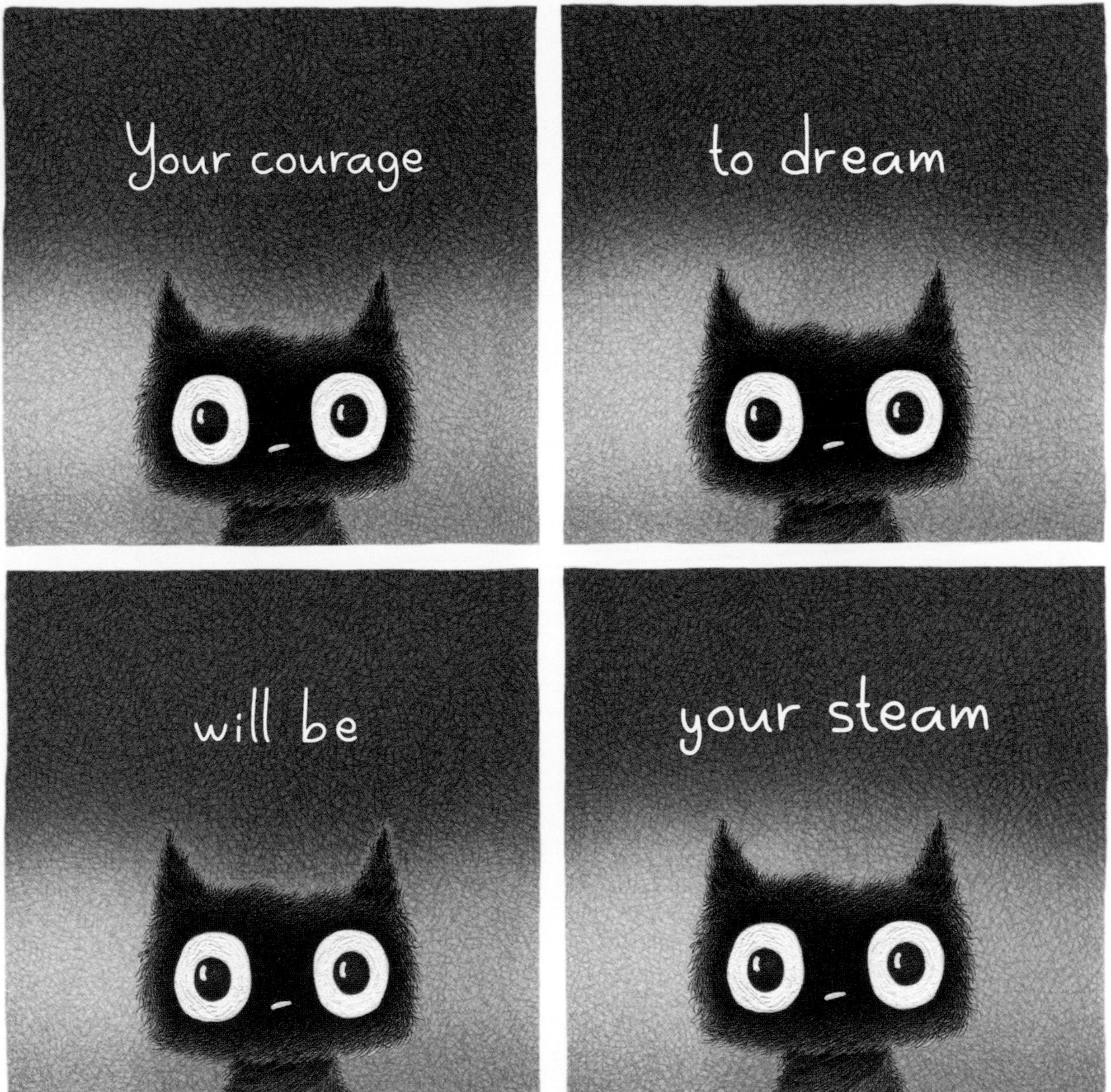
Your courage
to dream
will be
your steam

When touch is wrong
the bite is strong
when touch is right
I still might bite

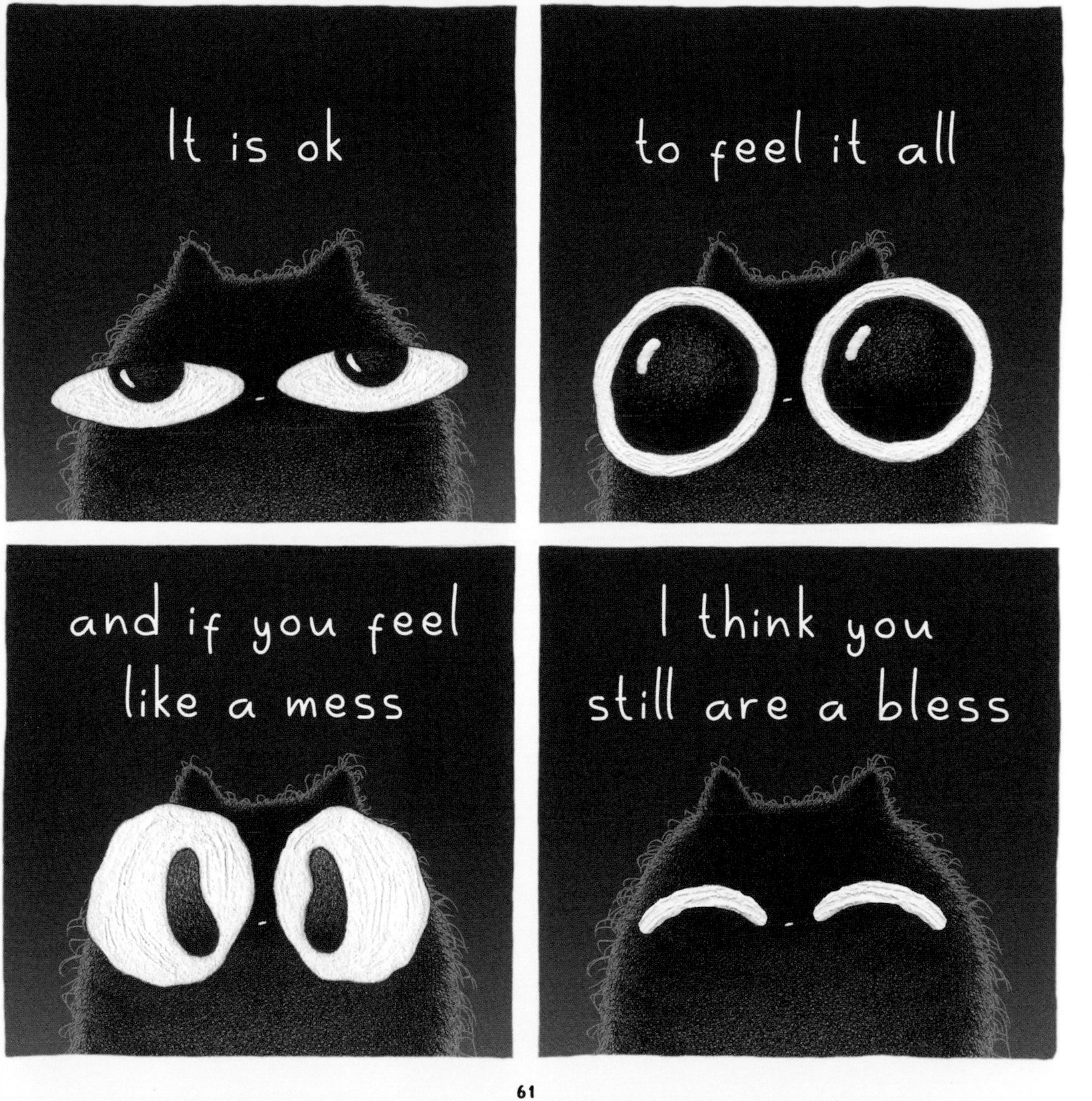
It is ok
to feel it all
and if you feel like a mess
I think you still are a bless

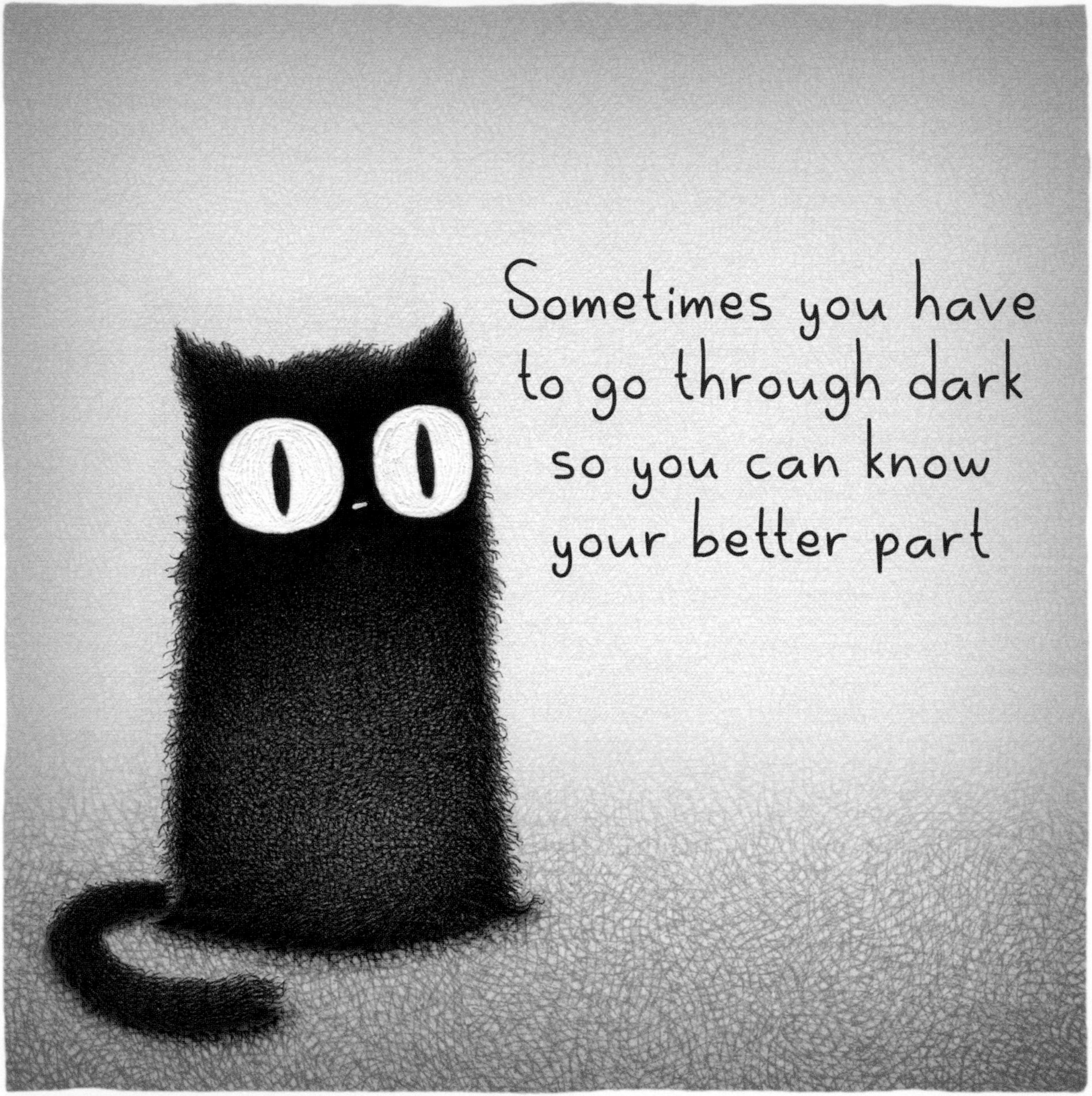
Sometimes you have
to go through dark
so you can know
your better part

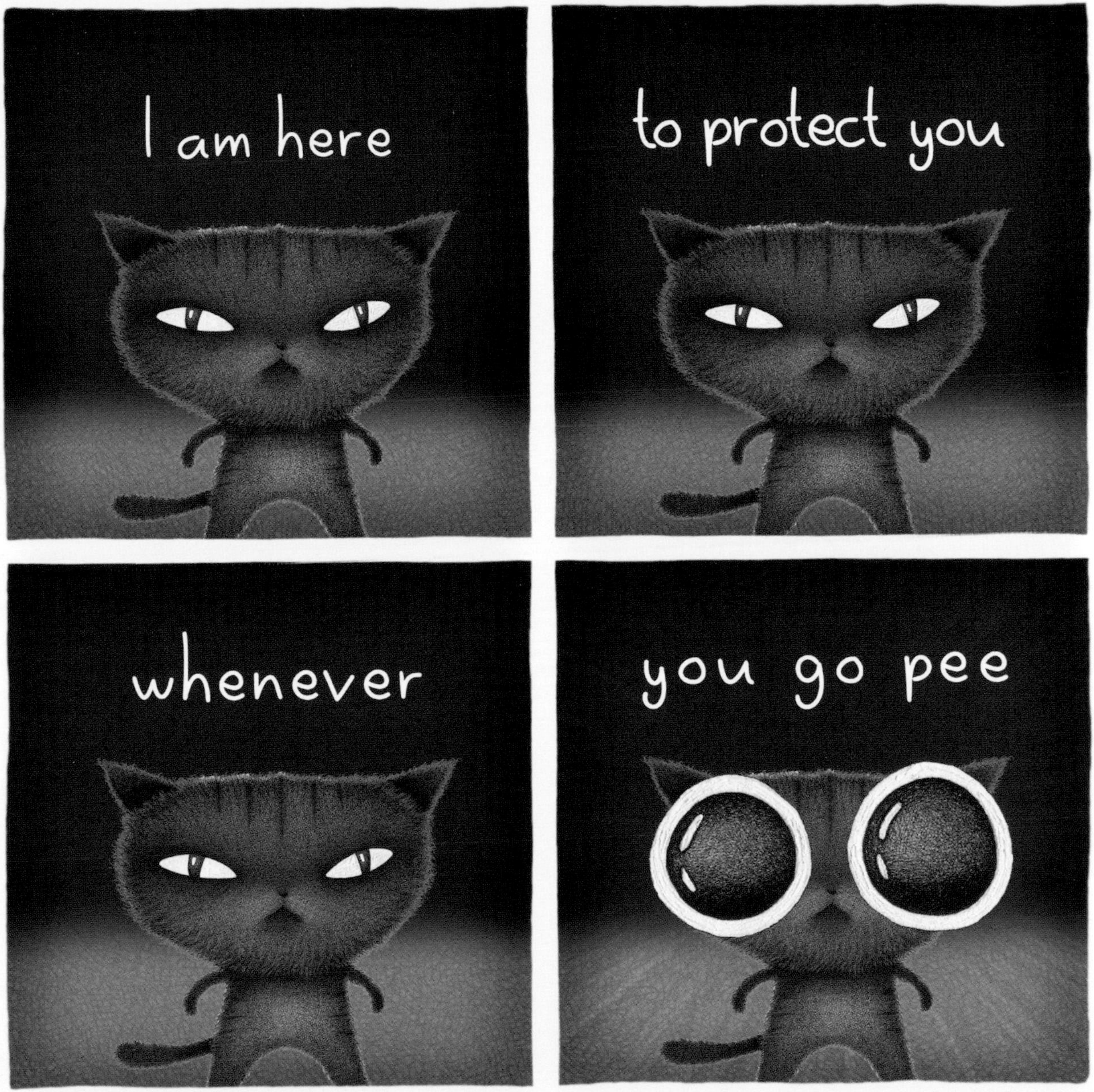
I am here
to protect you
whenever
you go pee

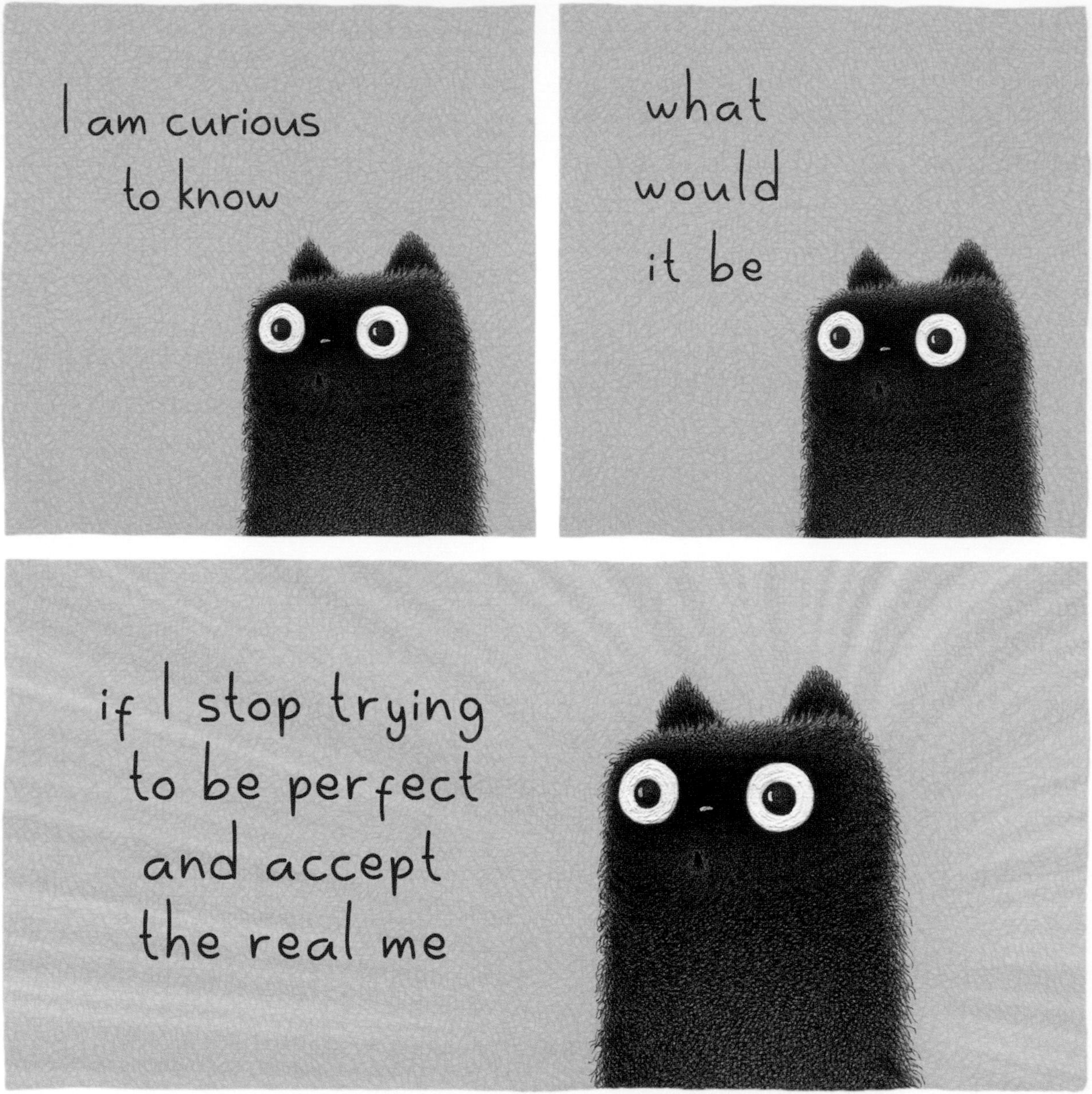
I am curious
to know
what
would
it be
if I stop trying
to be perfect
and accept
the real me

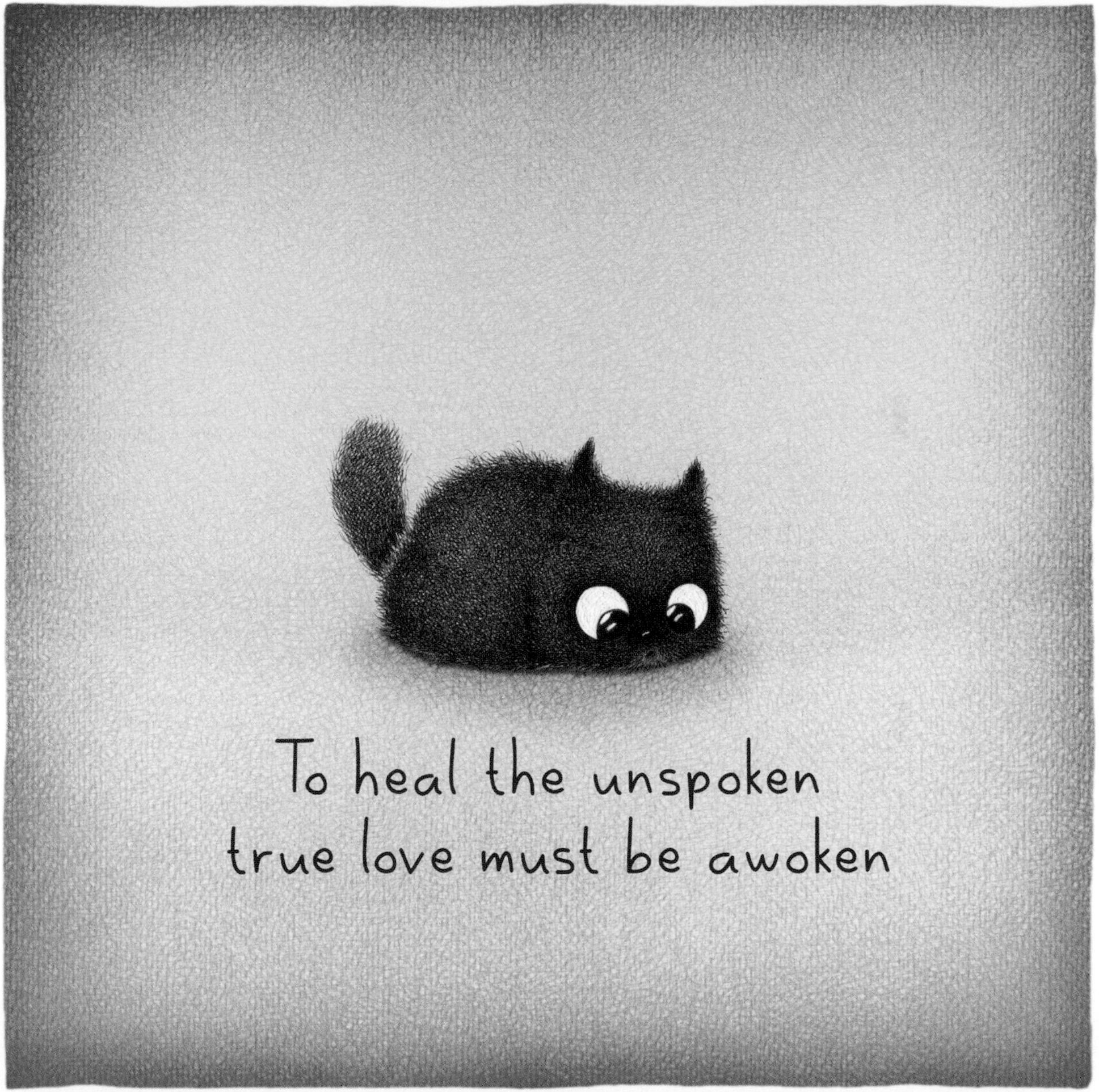
To heal the unspoken
true love must be awoken

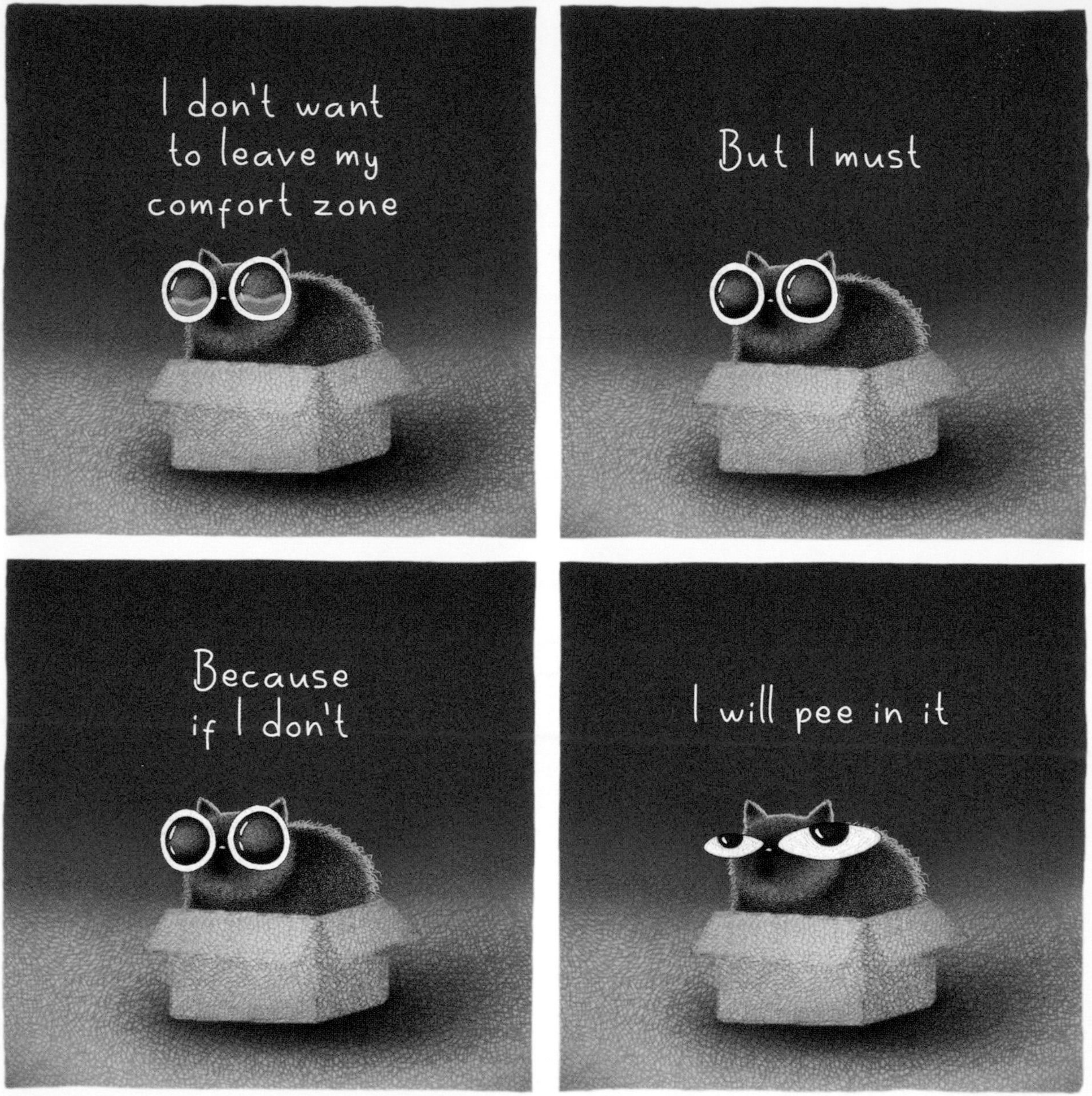
I don't want to leave my comfort zone
But I must
Because if I don't
I will pee in it

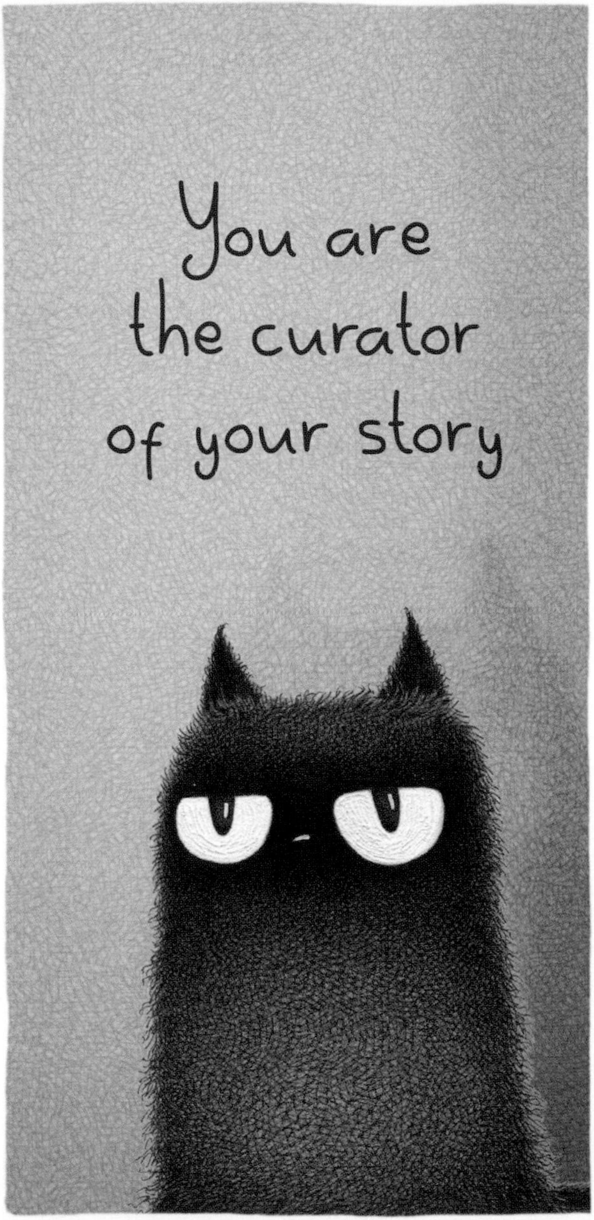
You are
the curator
of your story

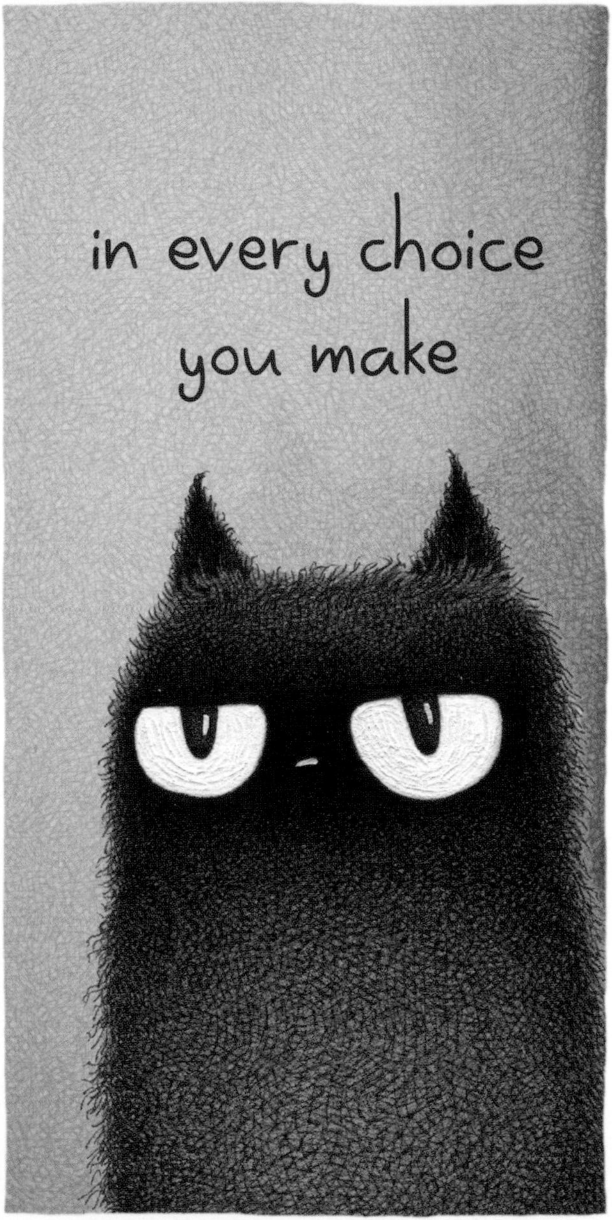
in every choice
you make

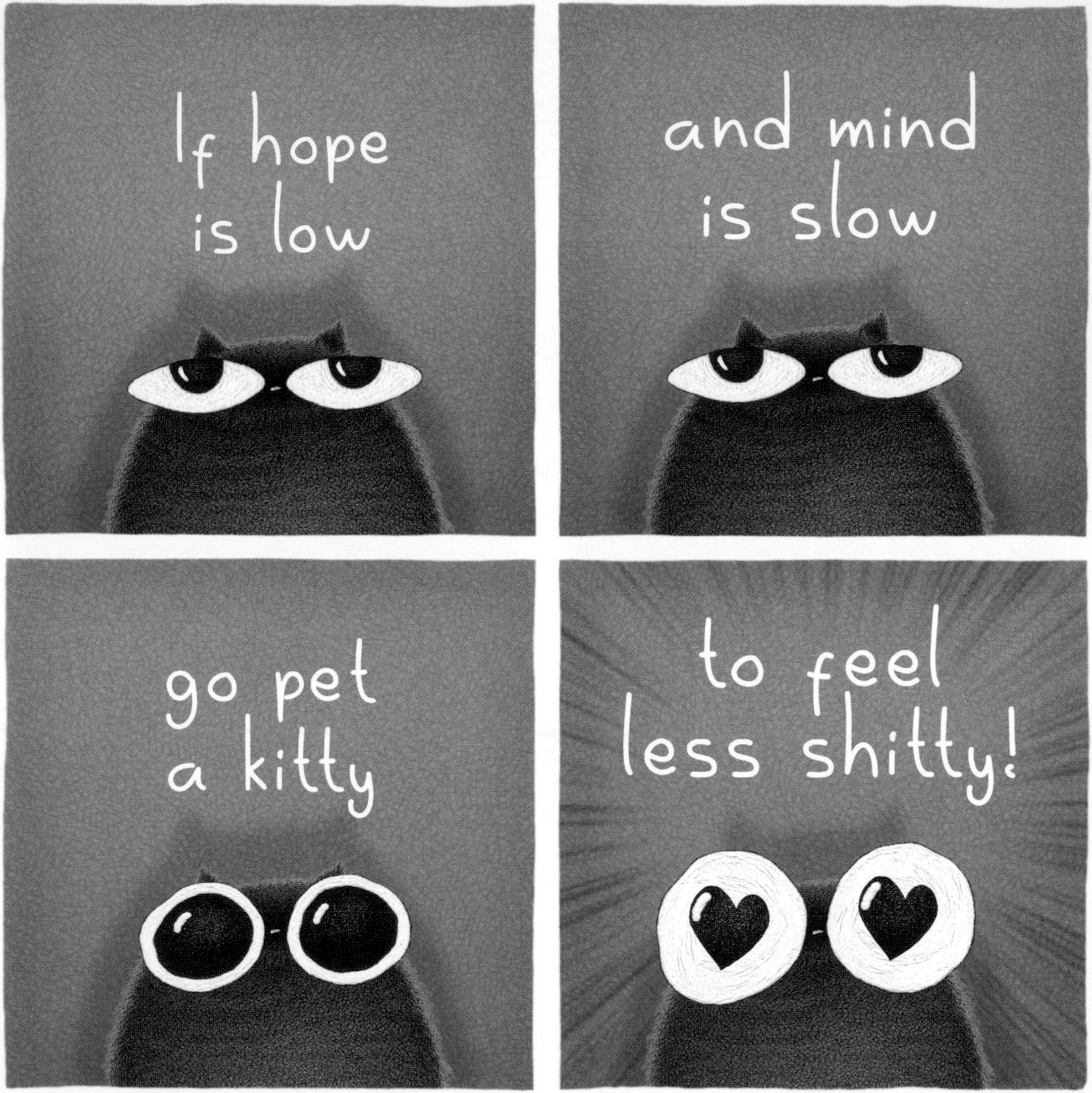
If hope is low
and mind is slow
go pet a kitty
to feel less shitty!

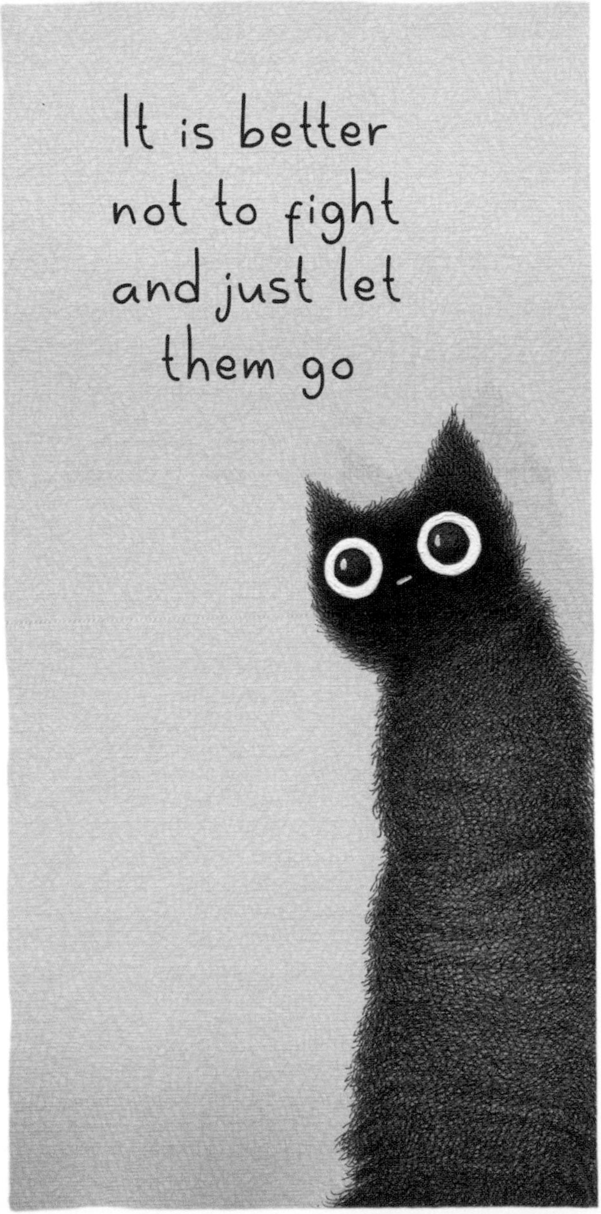
It is better
not to fight
and just let
them go

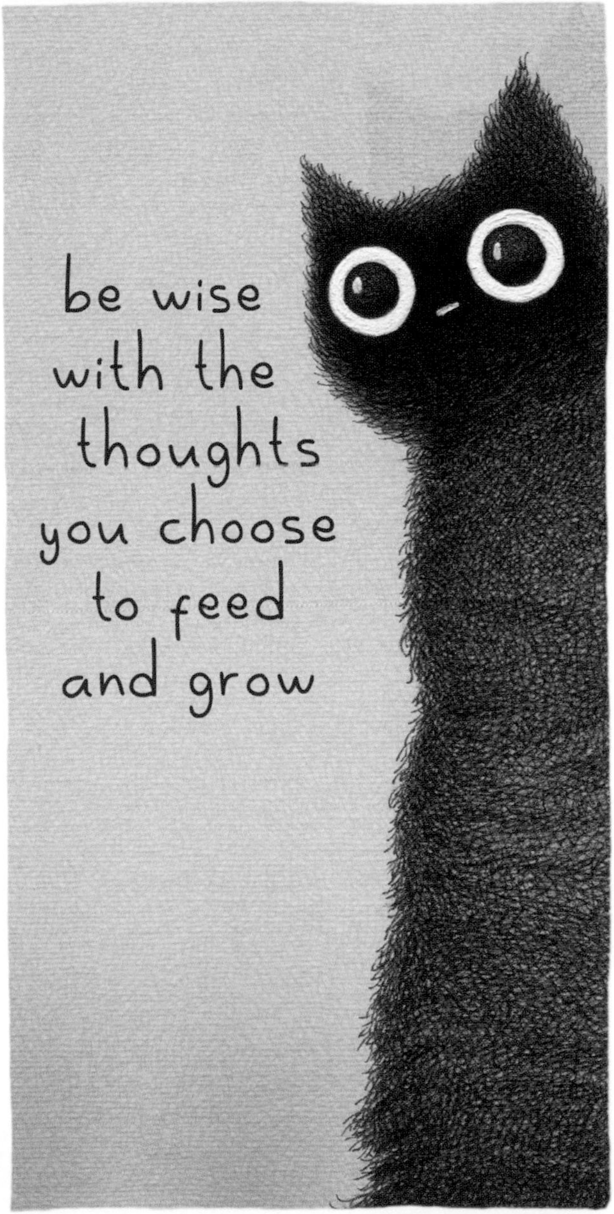
be wise
with the
thoughts
you choose
to feed
and grow

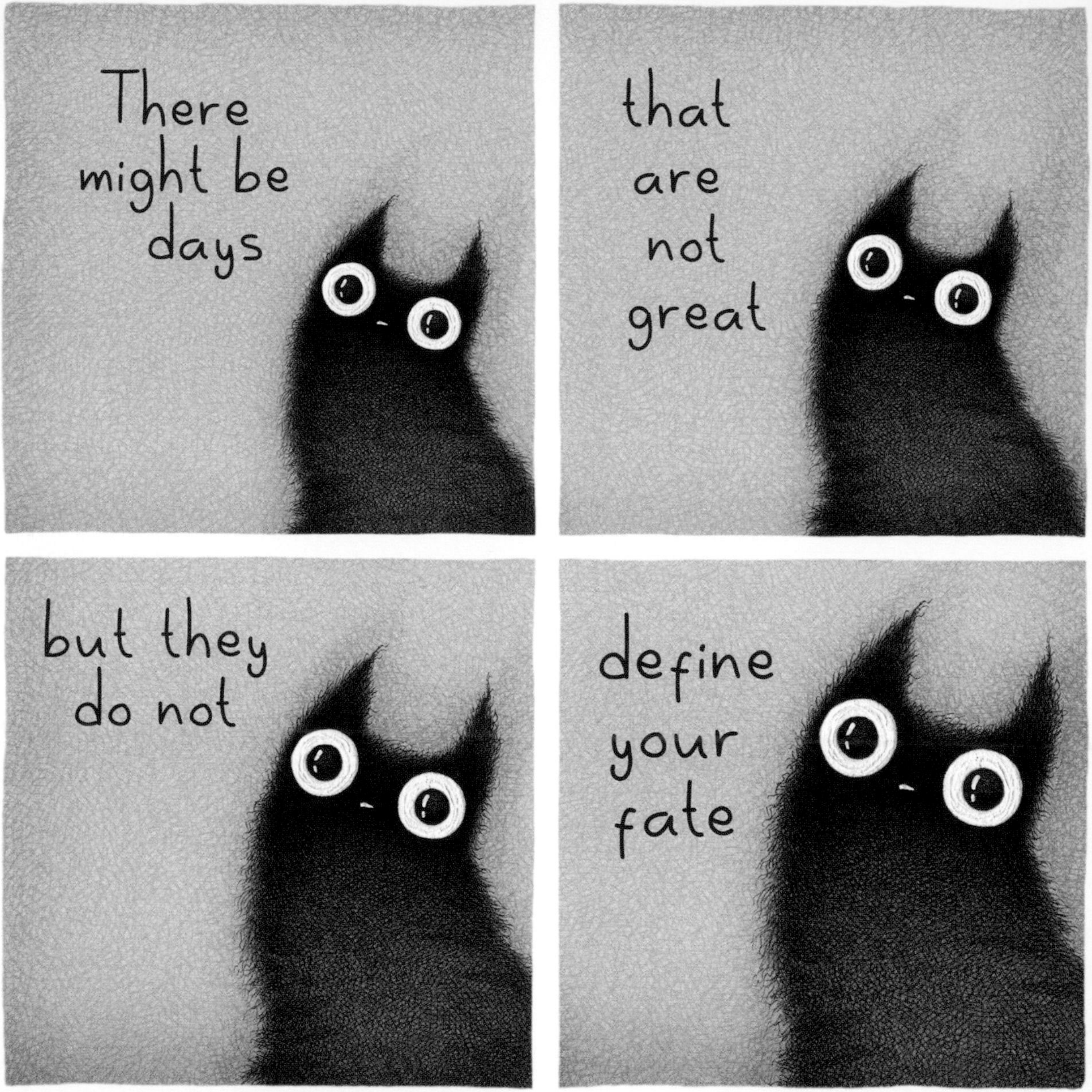
There might be days
that are not great
but they do not
define your fate

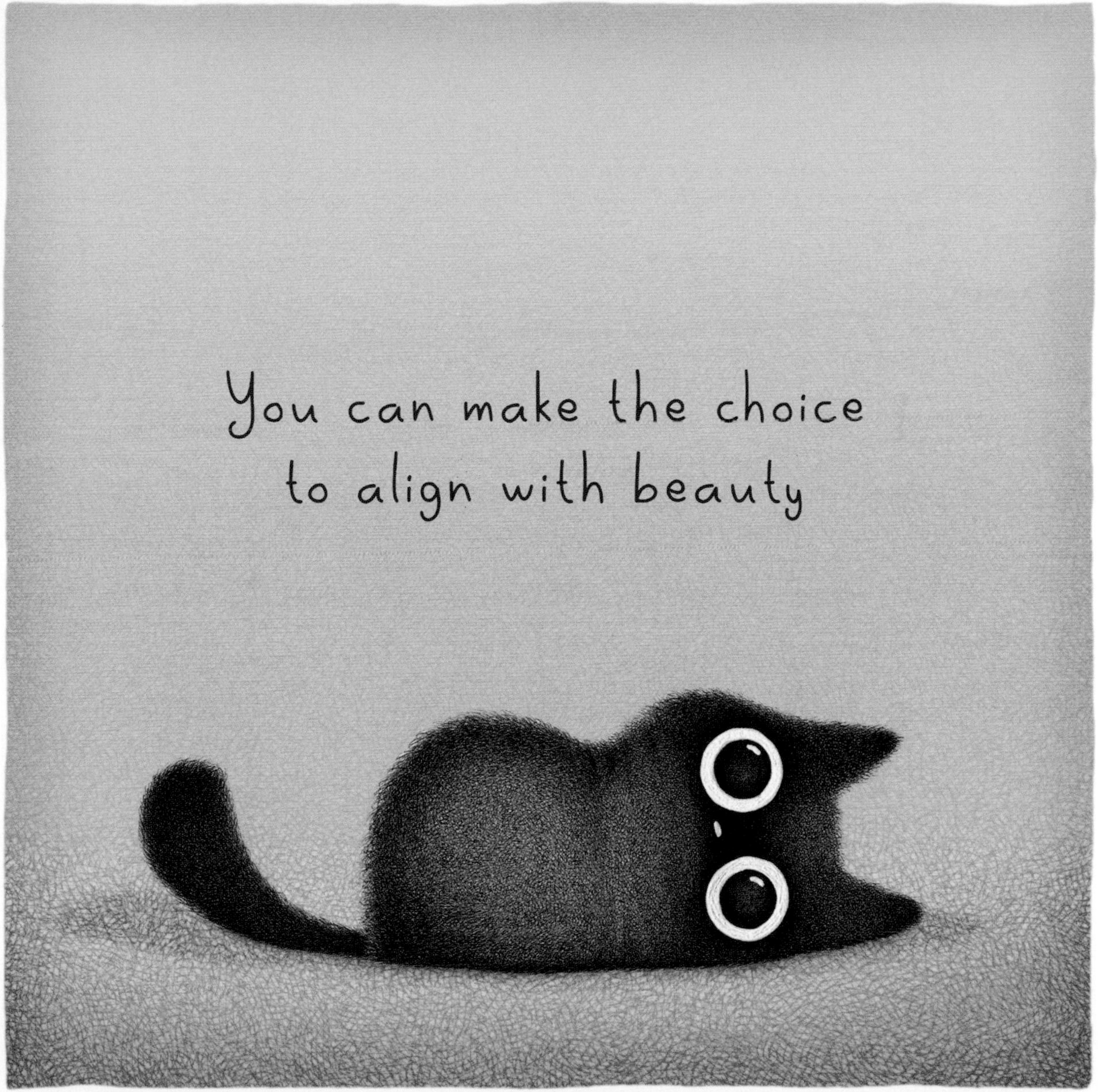
You can make the choice
to align with beauty

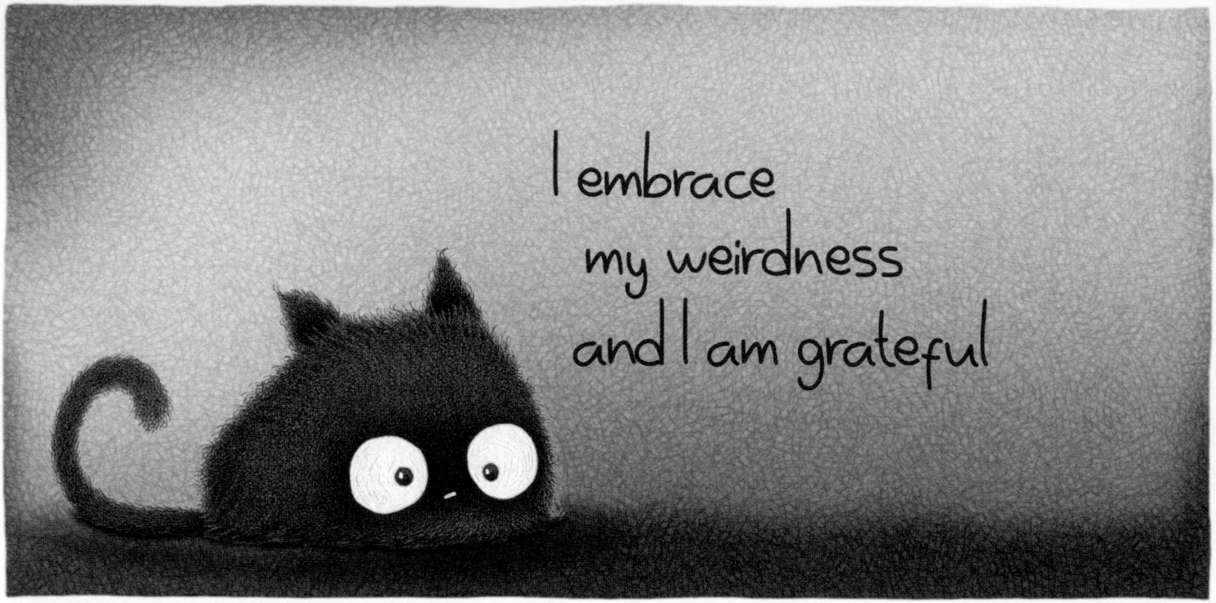
I embrace
my weirdness
and I am grateful

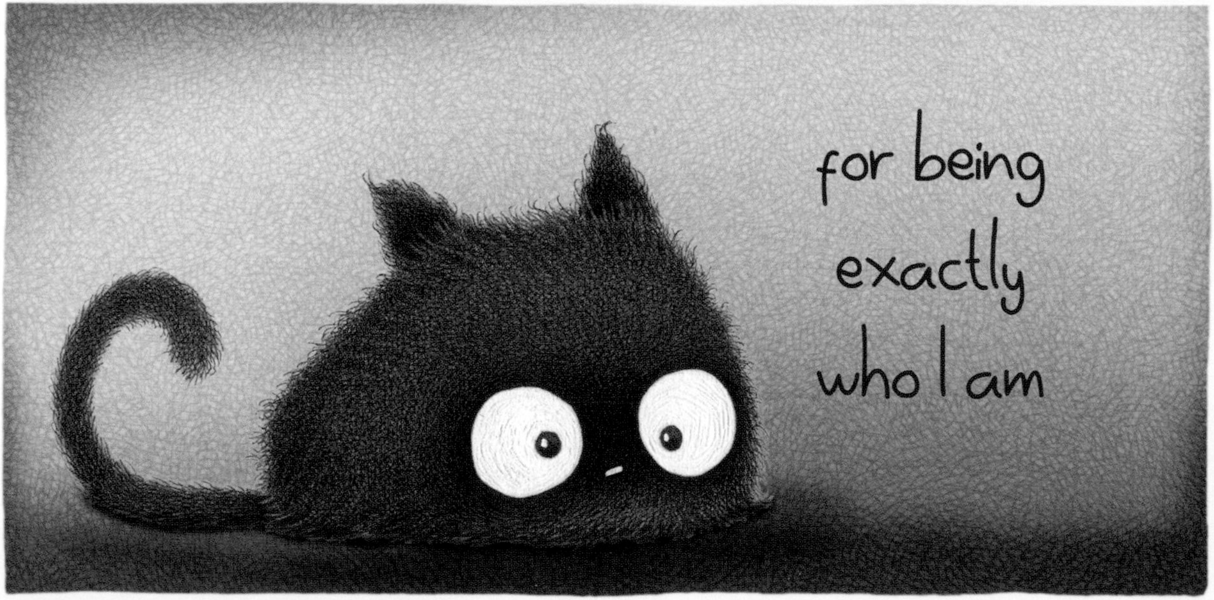
for being
exactly
who I am

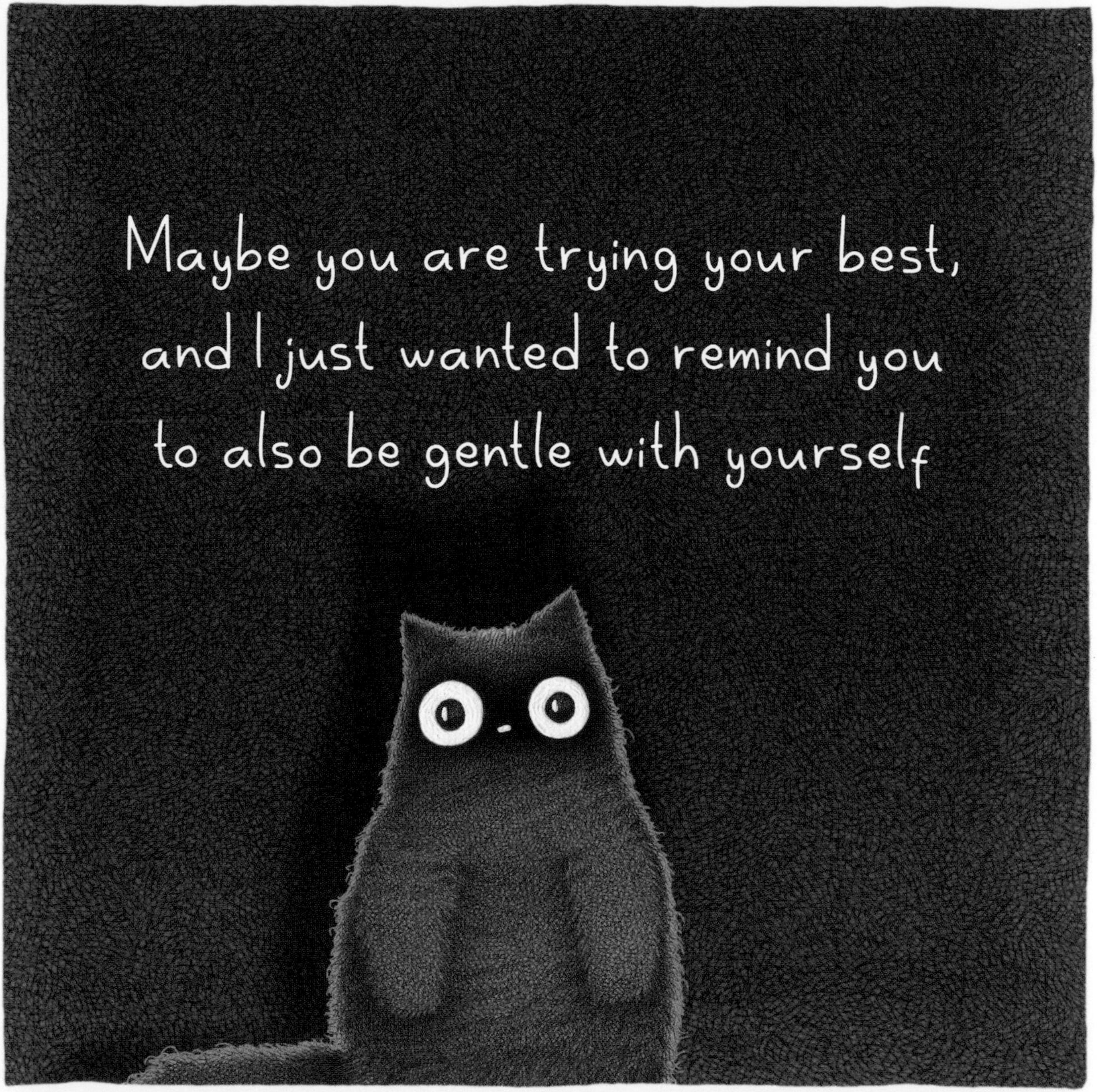
Maybe you are trying your best,
and I just wanted to remind you
to also be gentle with yourself

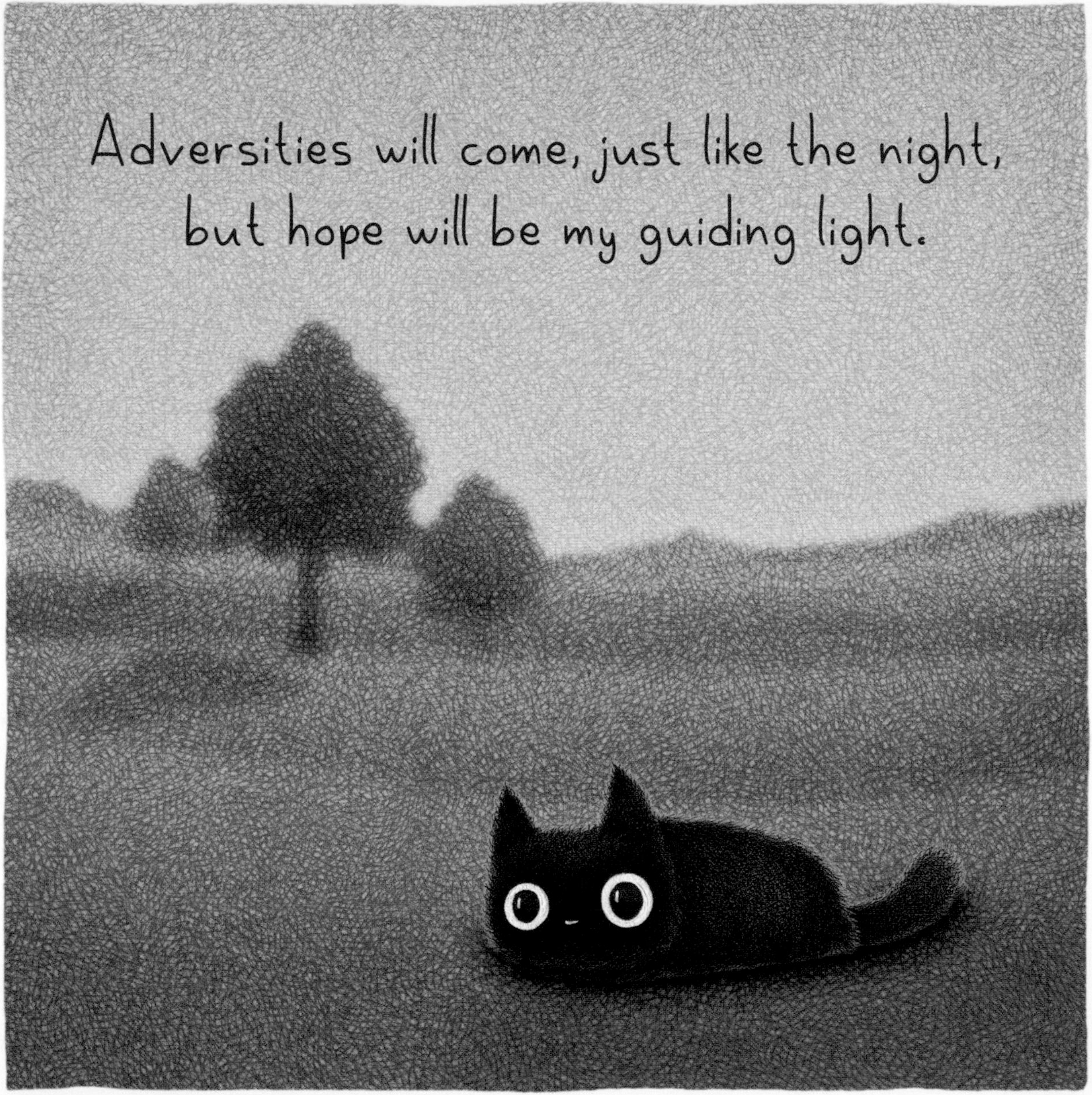
Adversities will come, just like the night,
but hope will be my guiding light.

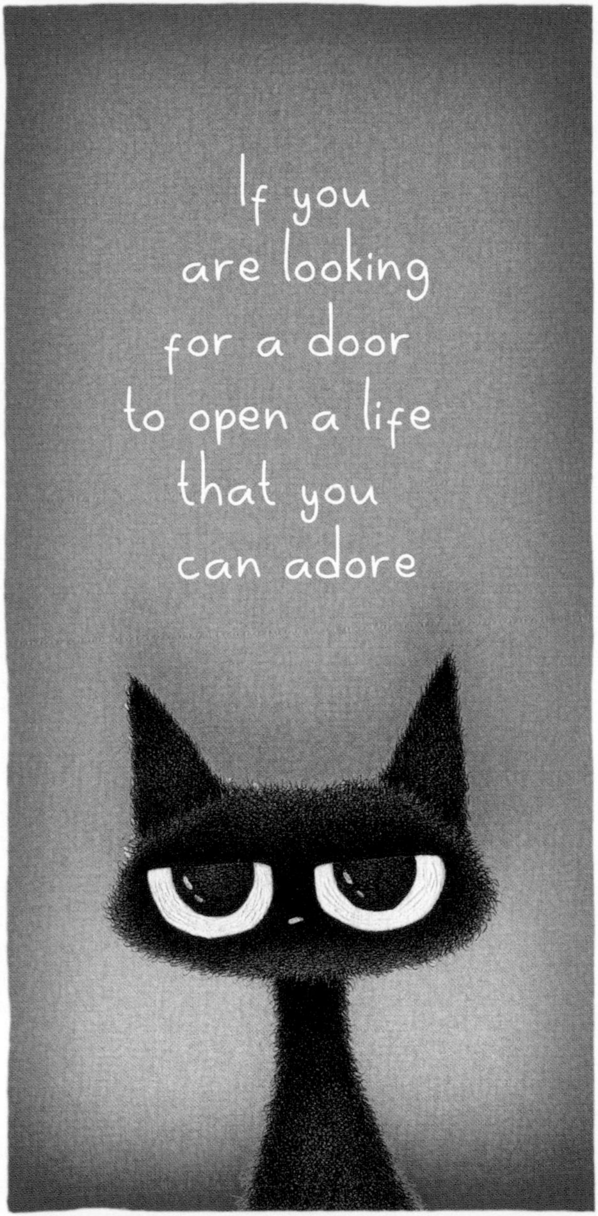
If you
are looking
for a door
to open a life
that you
can adore

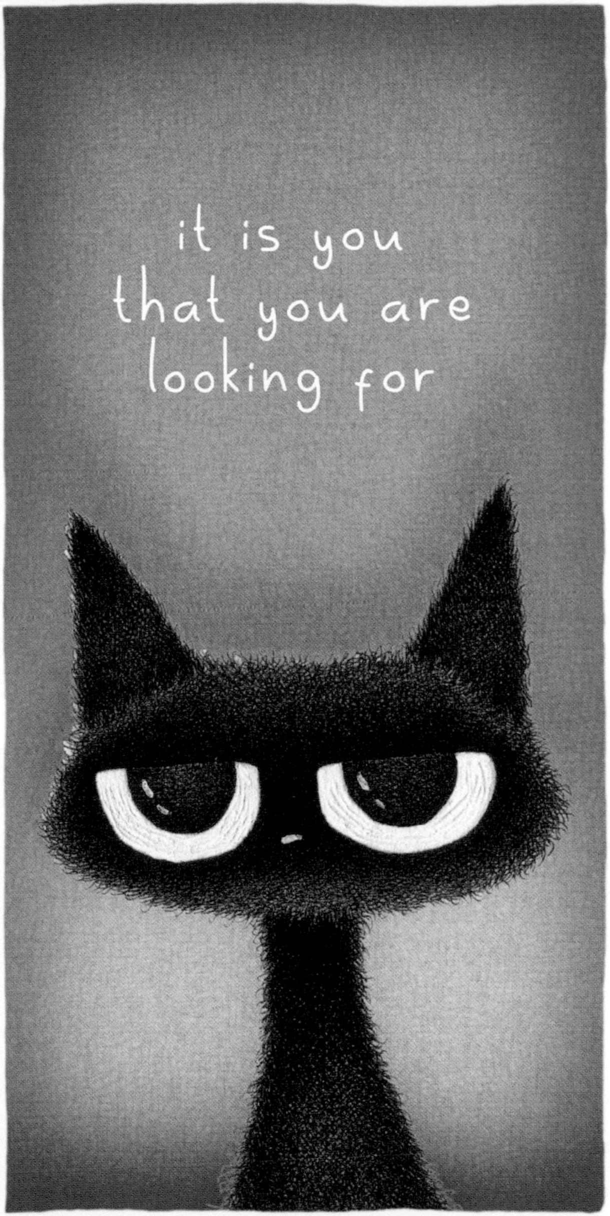
it is you
that you are
looking for

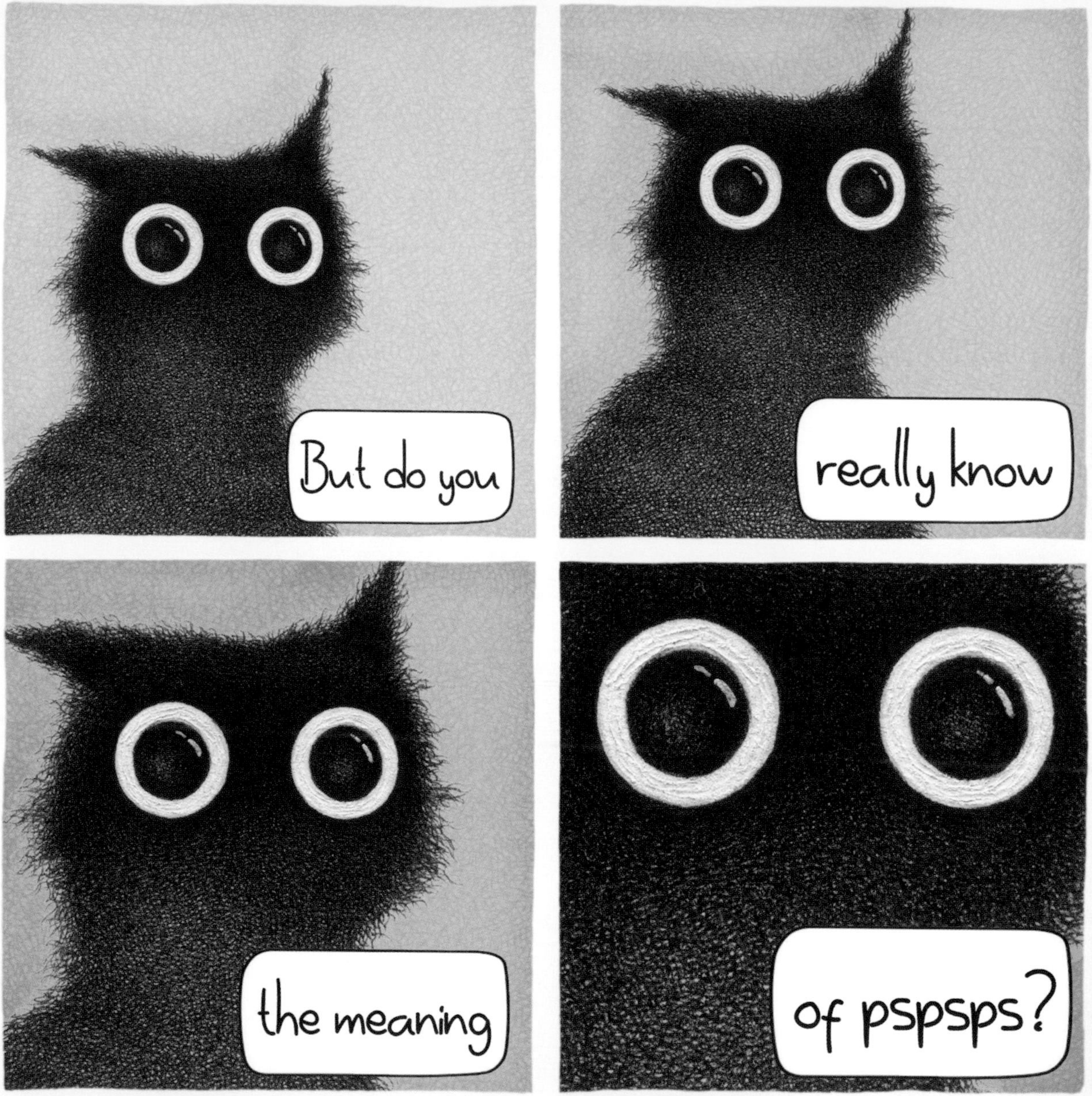
But do you
really know
the meaning
of pspsps?

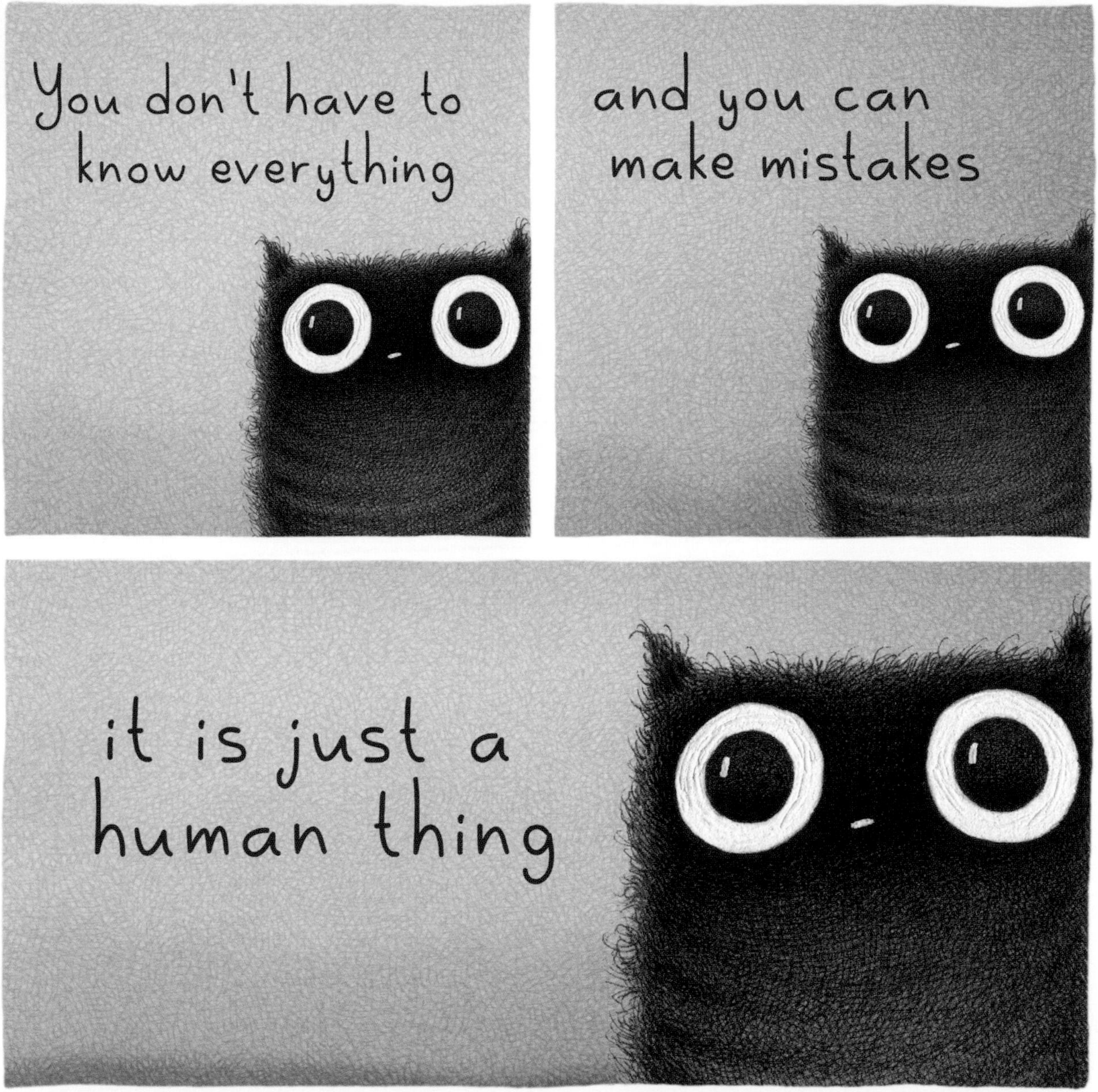
You don't have to know everything
and you can make mistakes
it is just a human thing

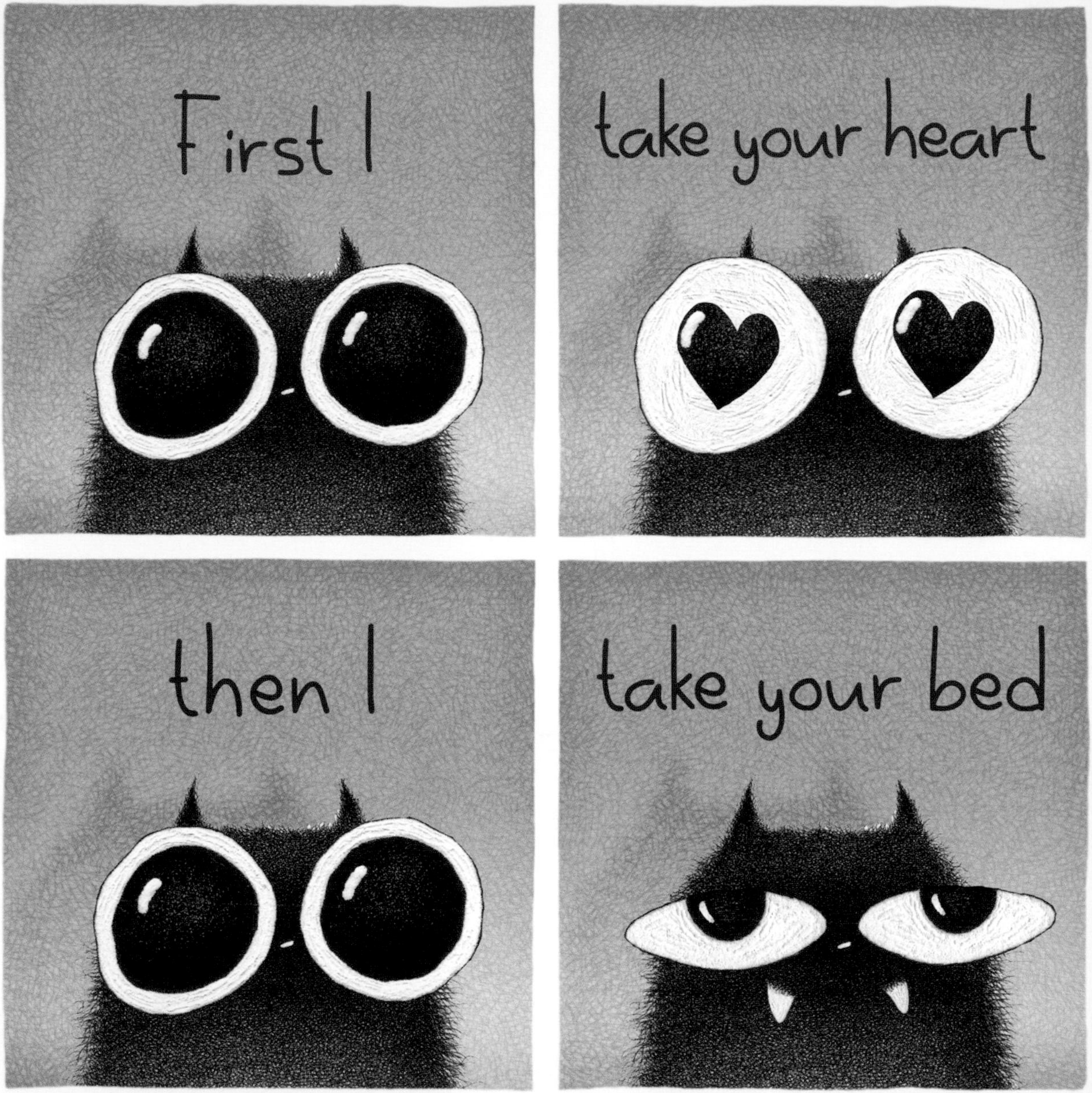
First I
take your heart
then I
take your bed

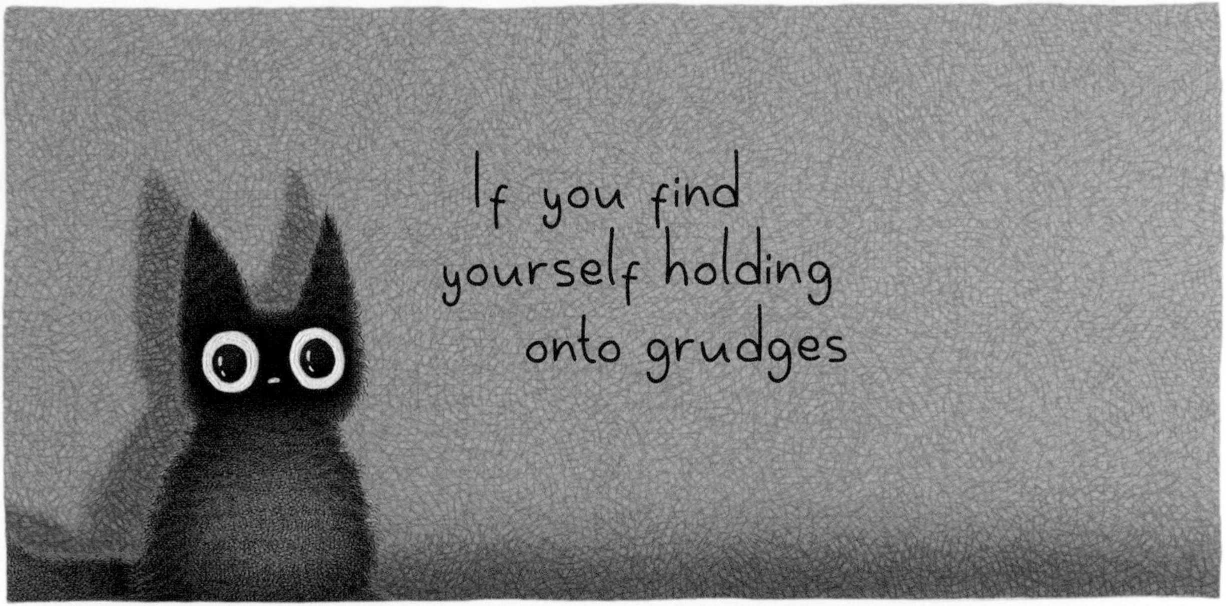
If you find
yourself holding
onto grudges

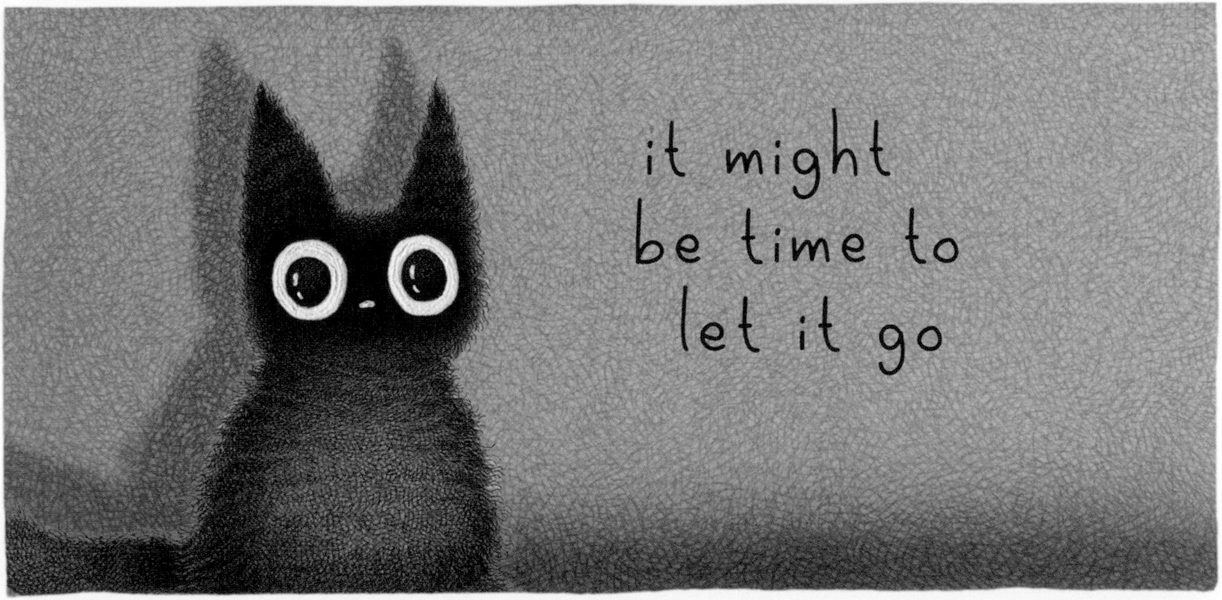
it might
be time to
let it go

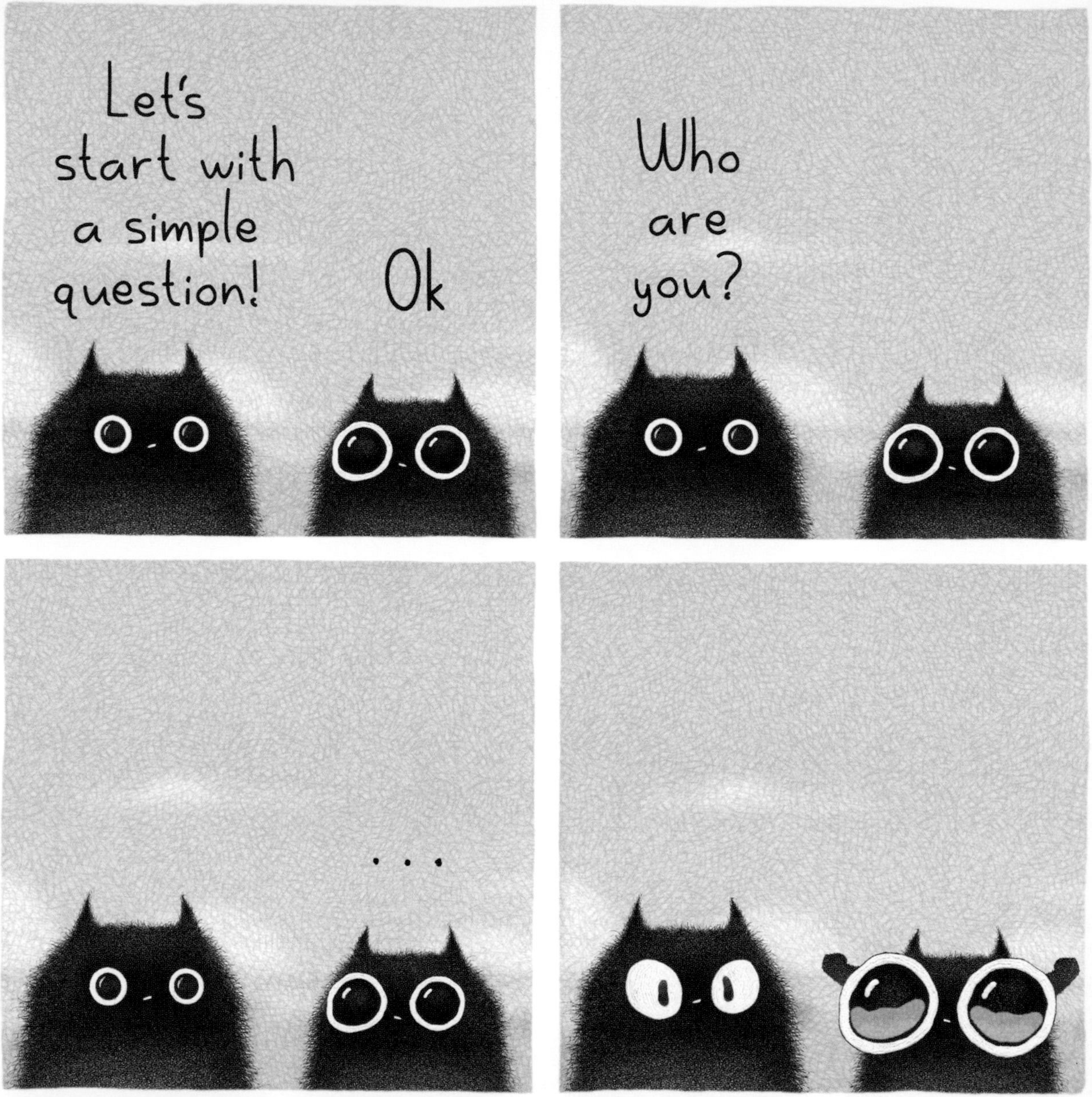
Let's start with a simple question!
Ok
Who are you?
. . .

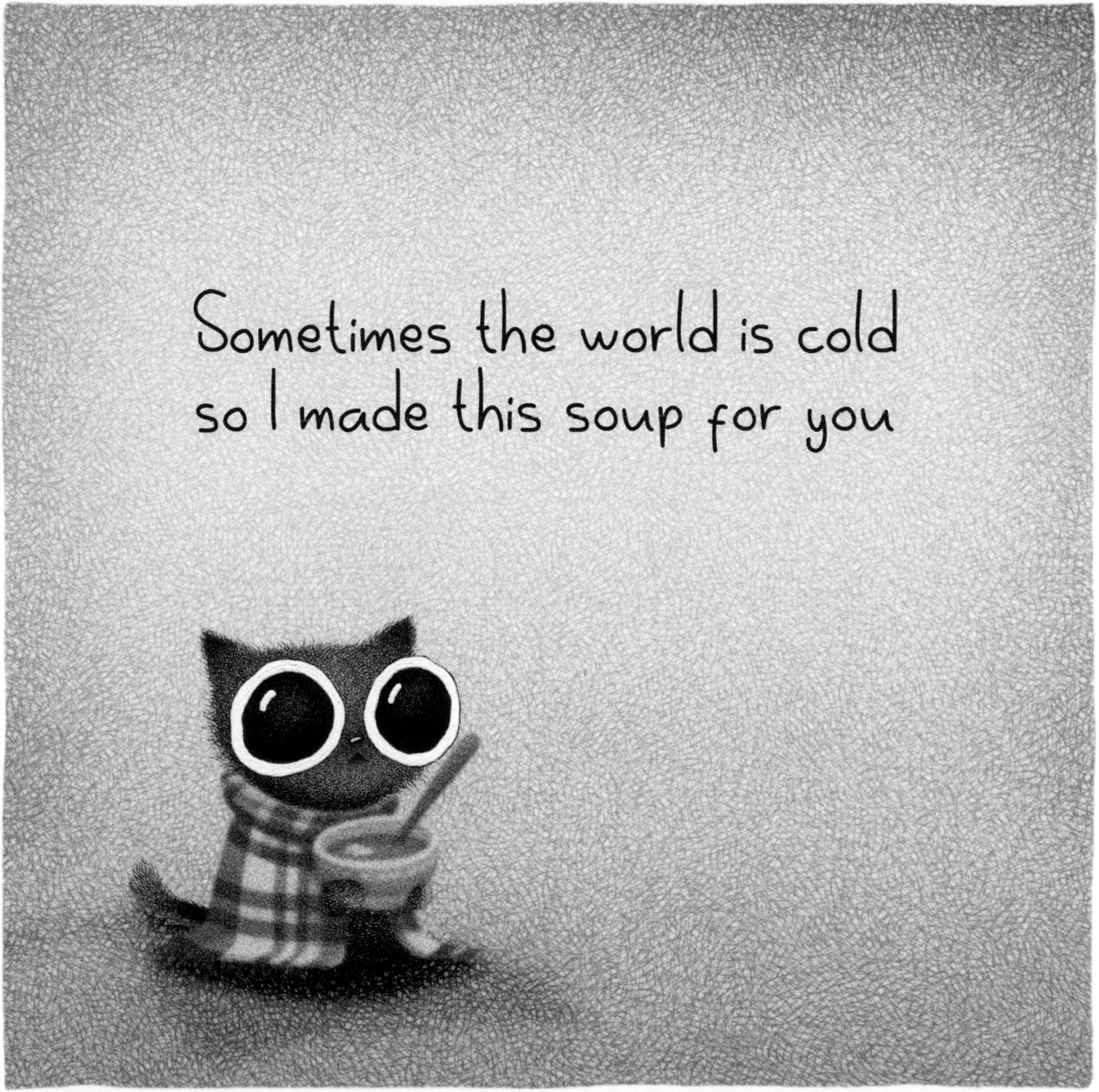
Sometimes the world is cold
so I made this soup for you

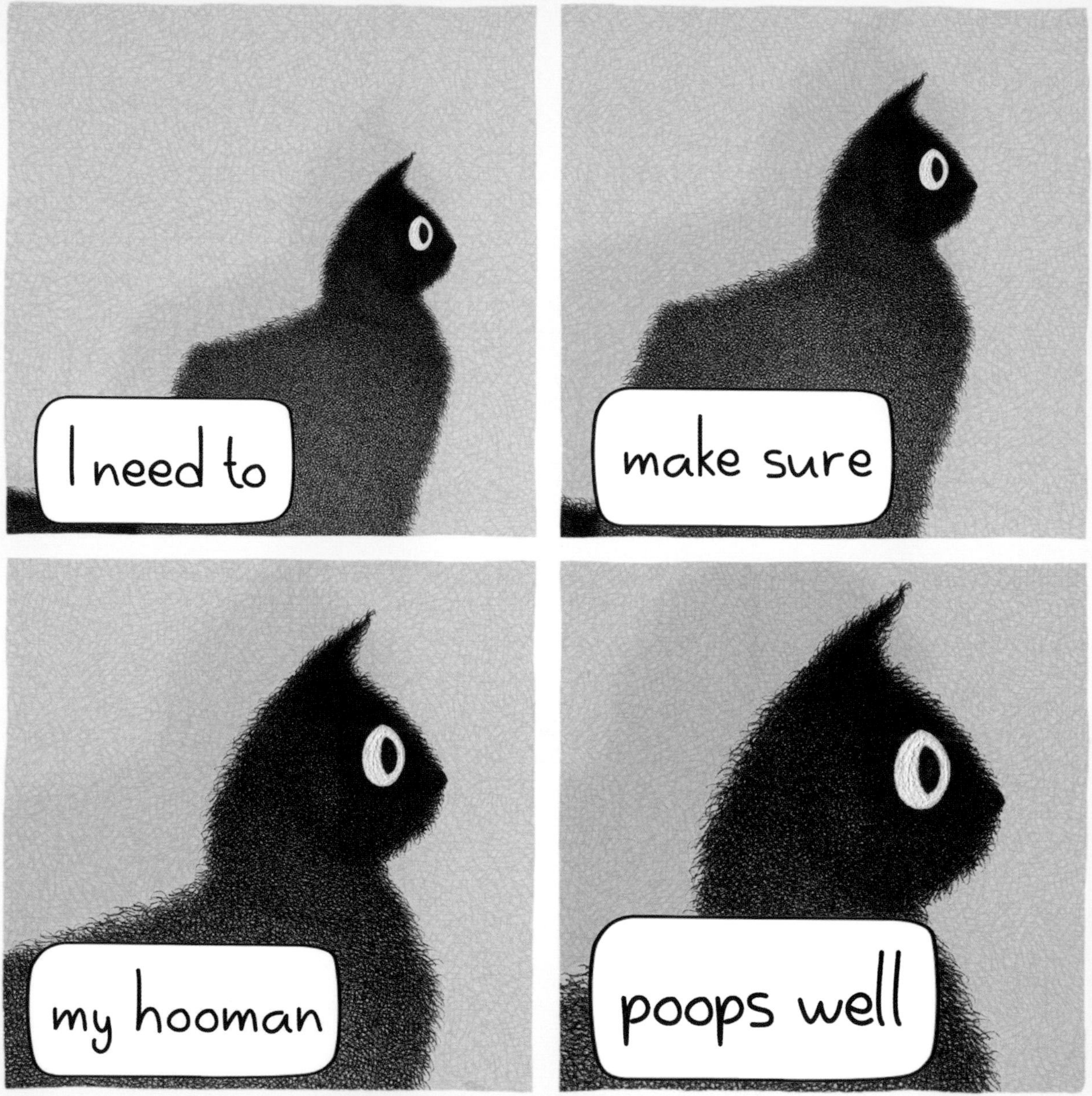
I need to
make sure
my hooman
poops well

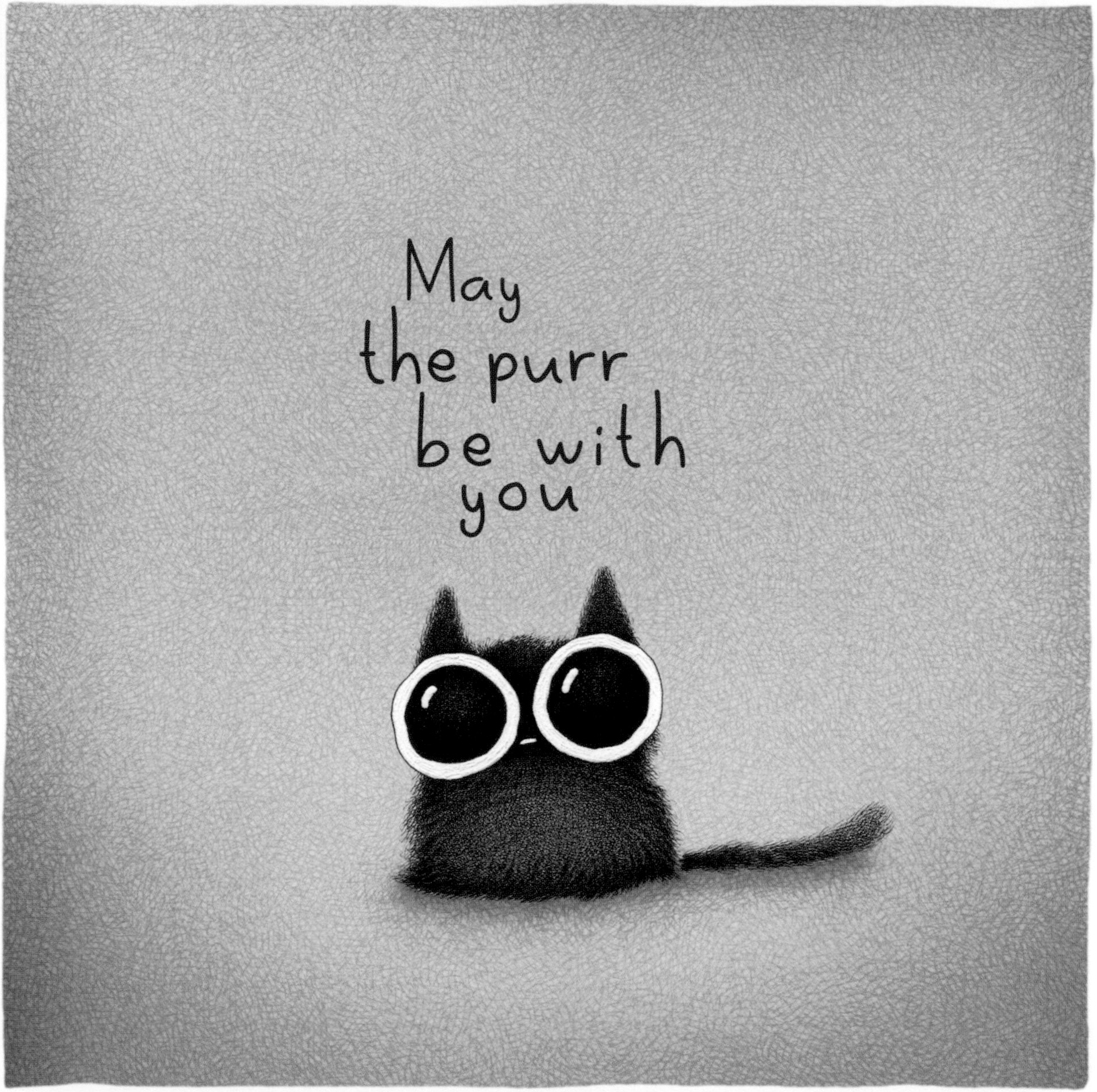
May the purr be with you

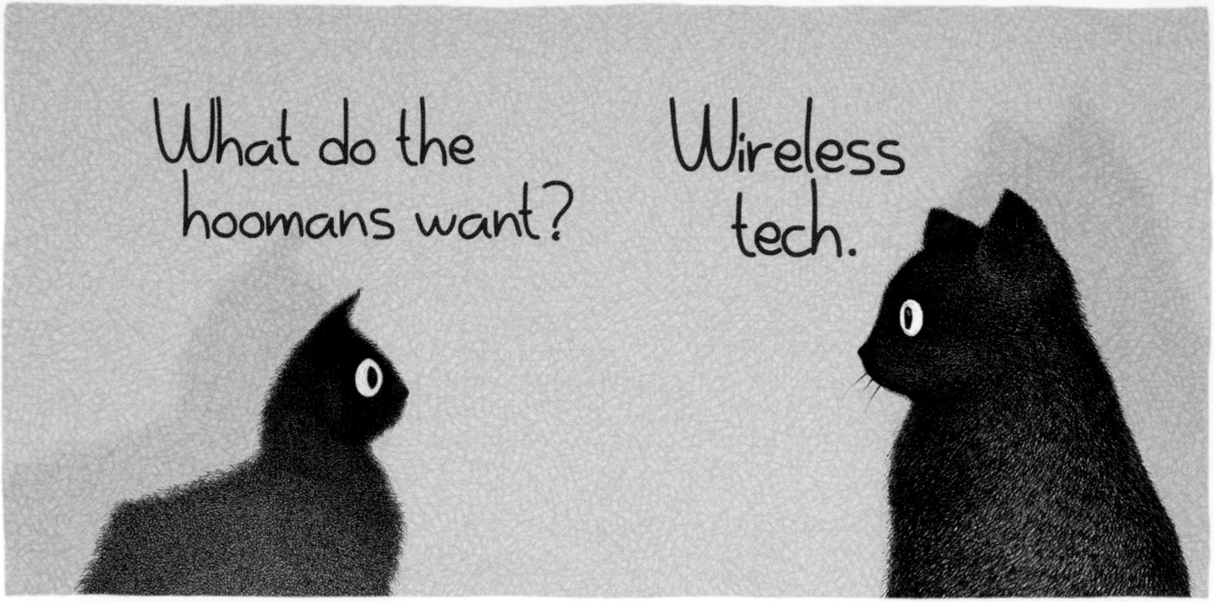
What do the hoomans want?
Wireless tech.

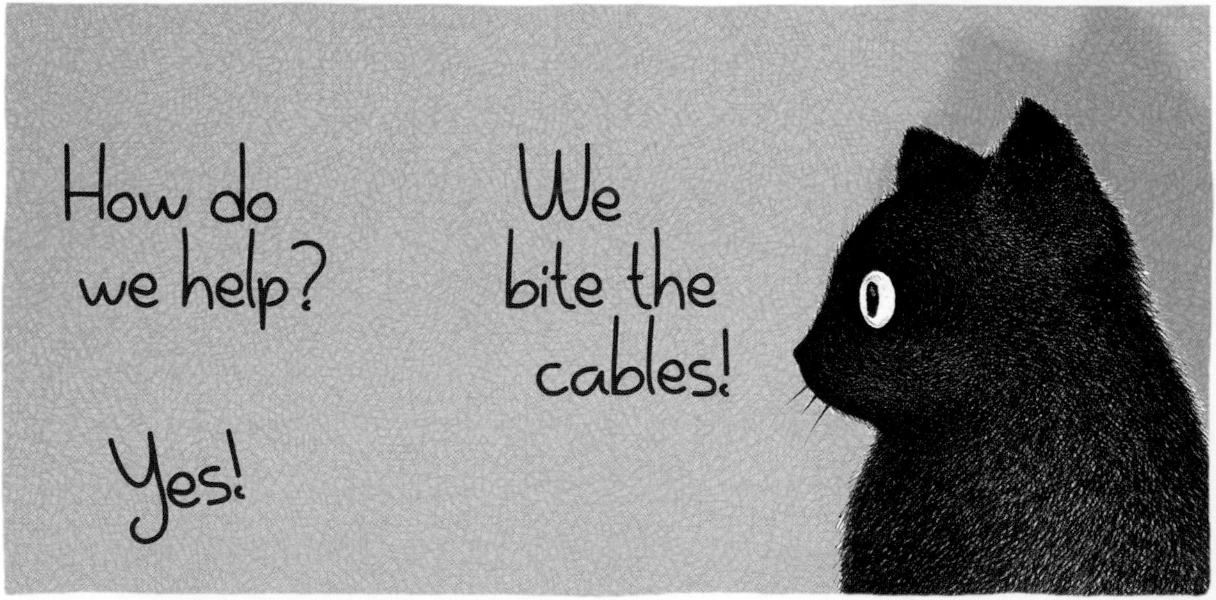
How do we help?
We bite the cables!
Yes!

Look into my eyes
and forget you
already fed me

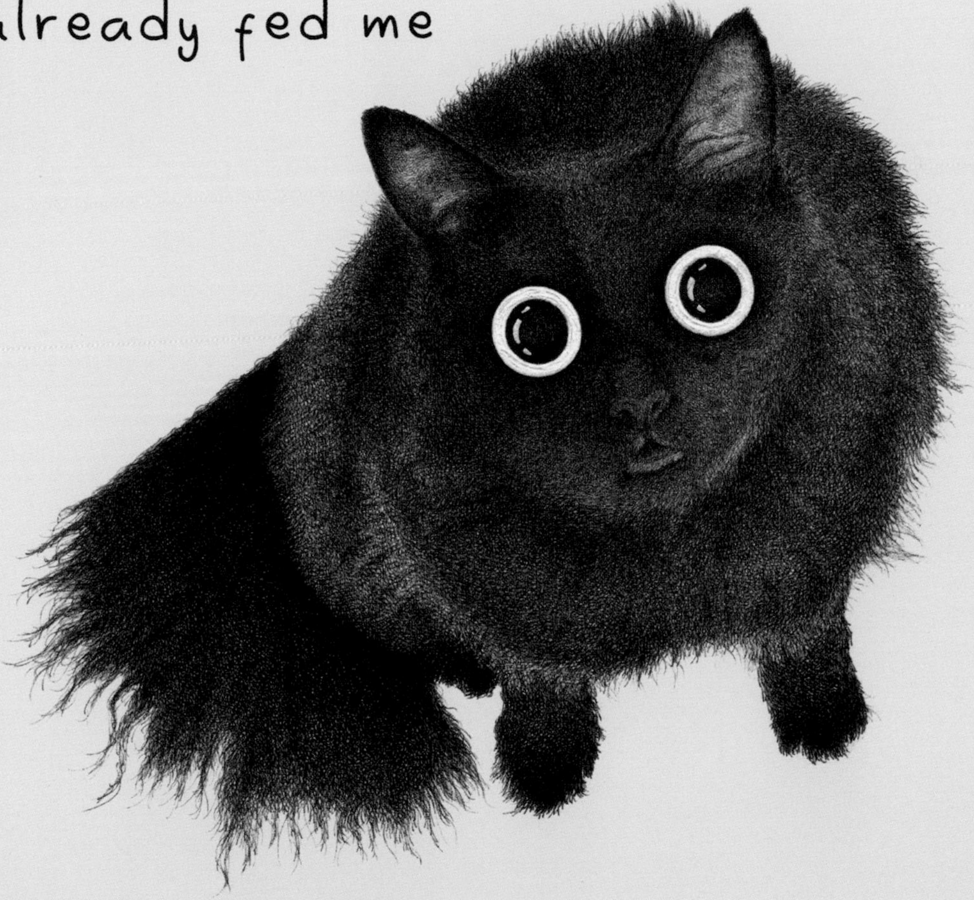

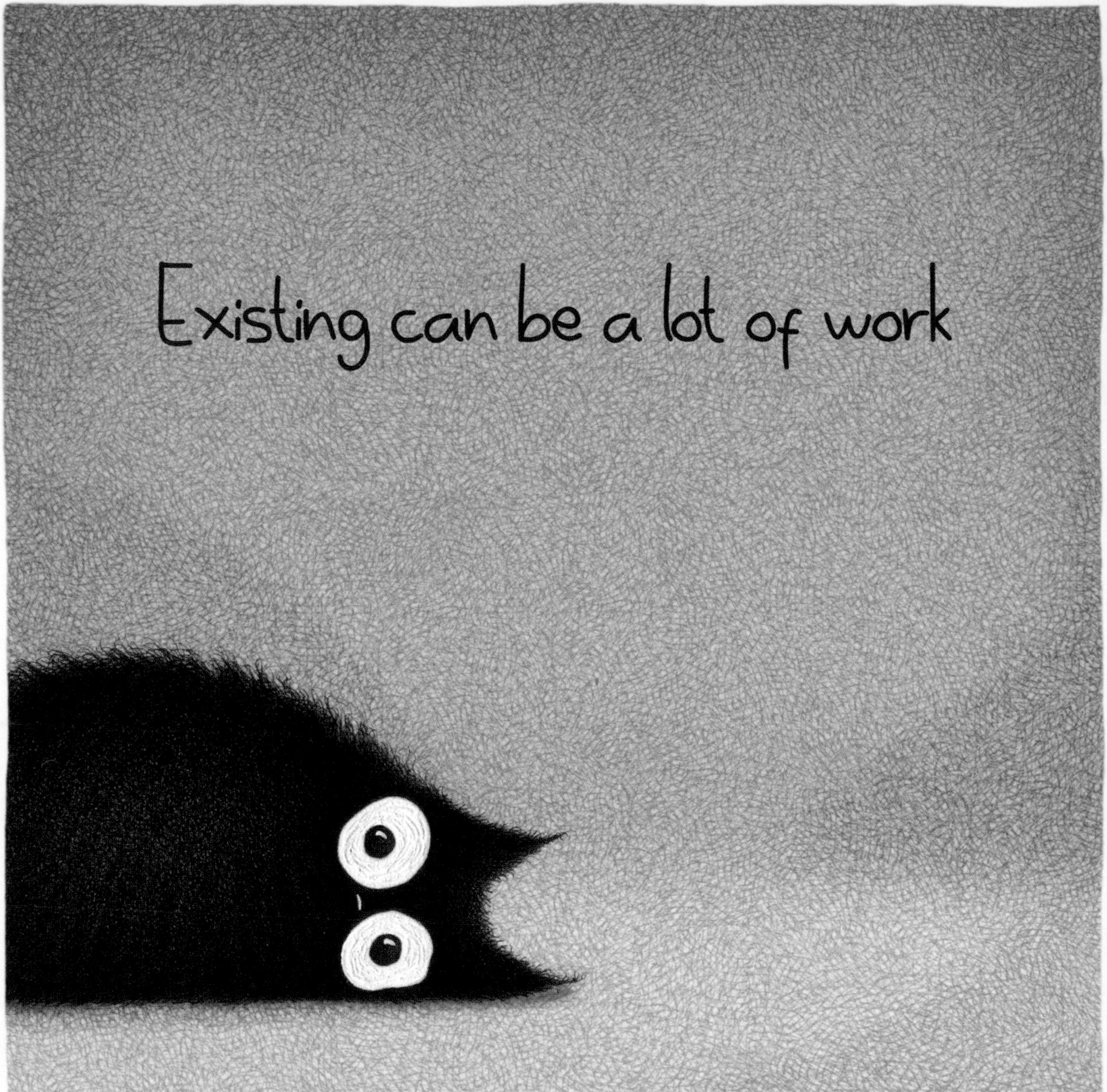
Existing can be a lot of work

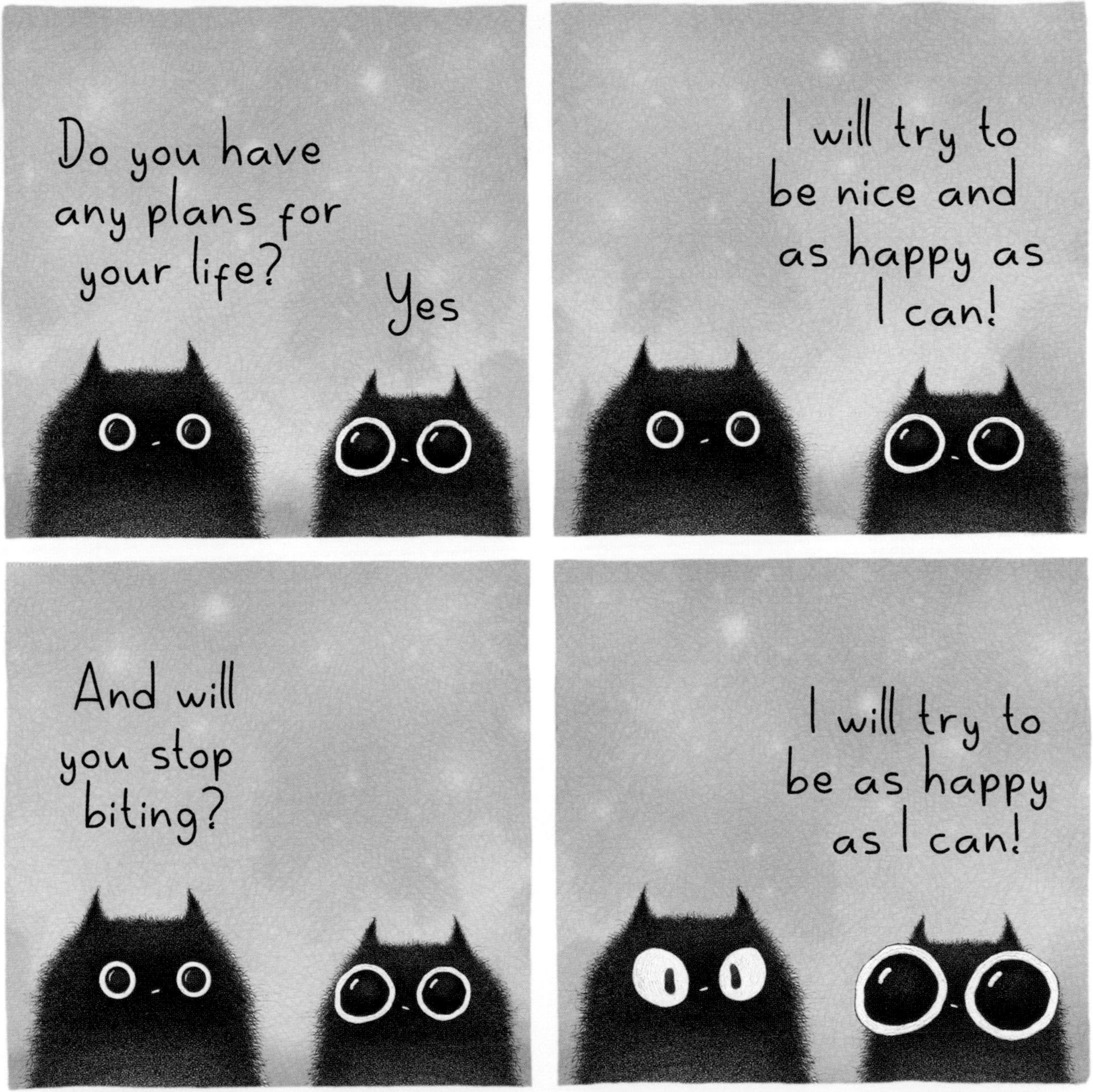
Do you have any plans for your life?
Yes
I will try to be nice and as happy as I can!
And will you stop biting?
I will try to be as happy as I can!

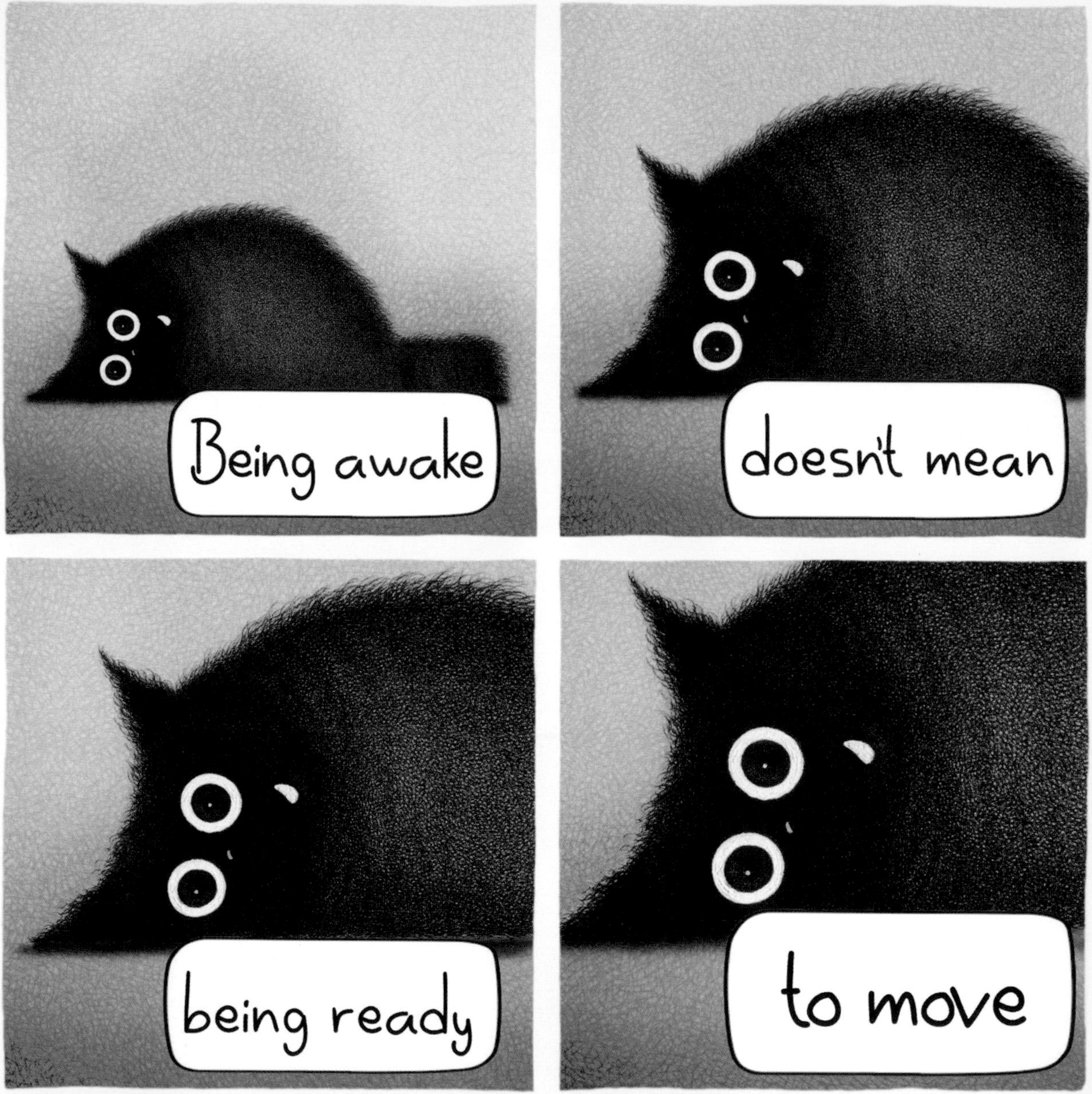
Being awake
doesn't mean
being ready
to move

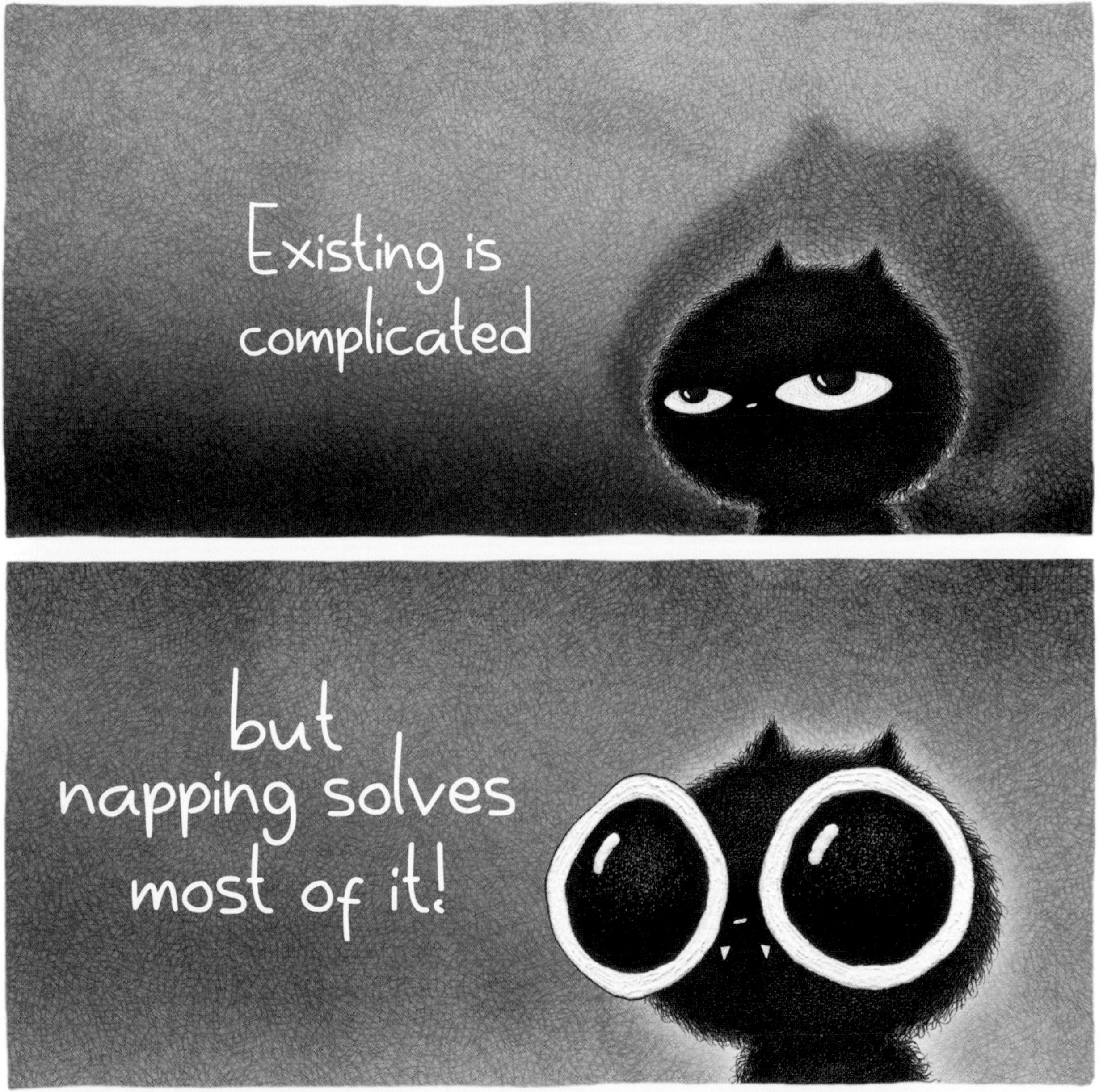
Existing is complicated
but napping solves most of it!

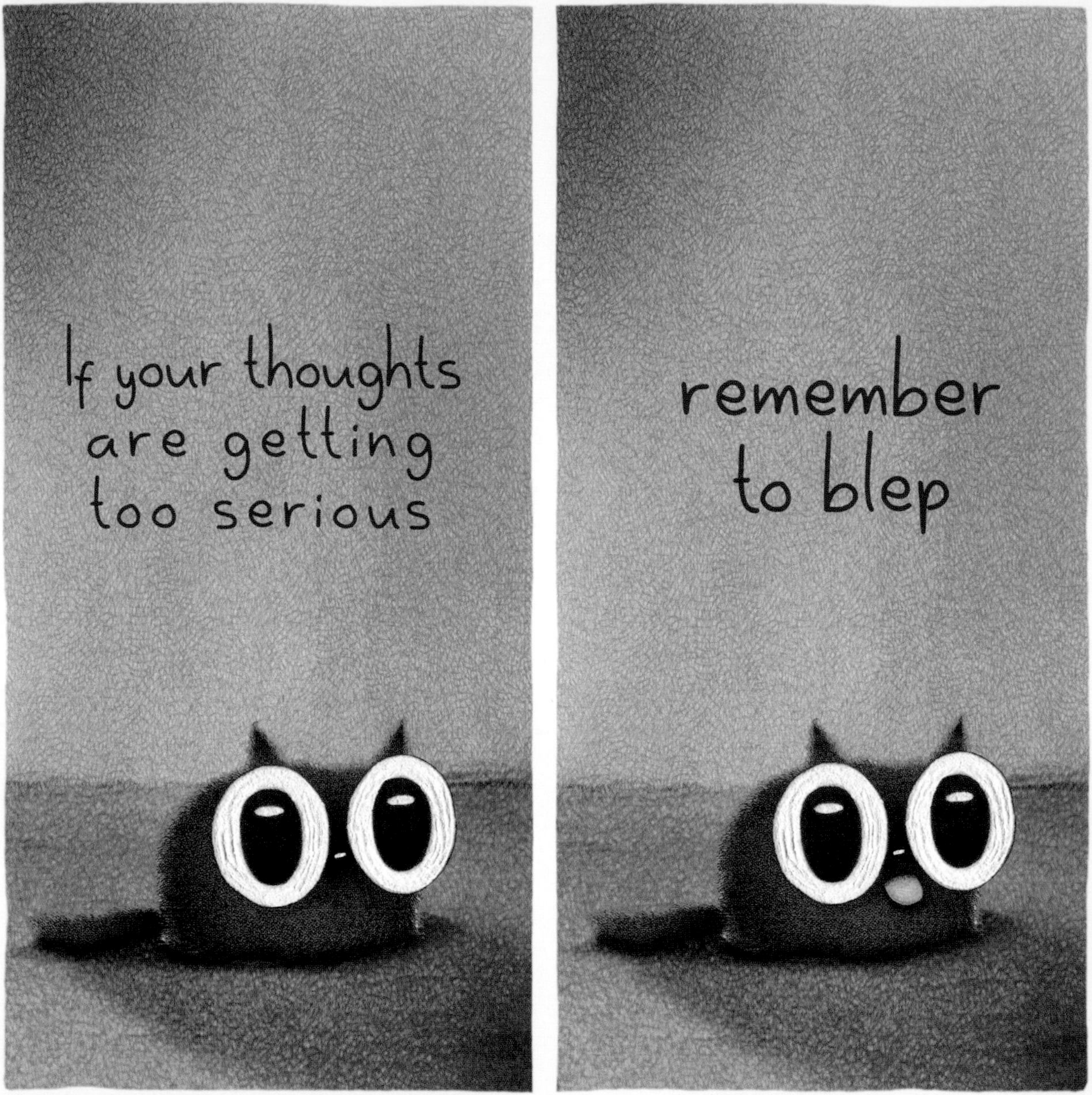
If your thoughts are getting too serious
remember to blep

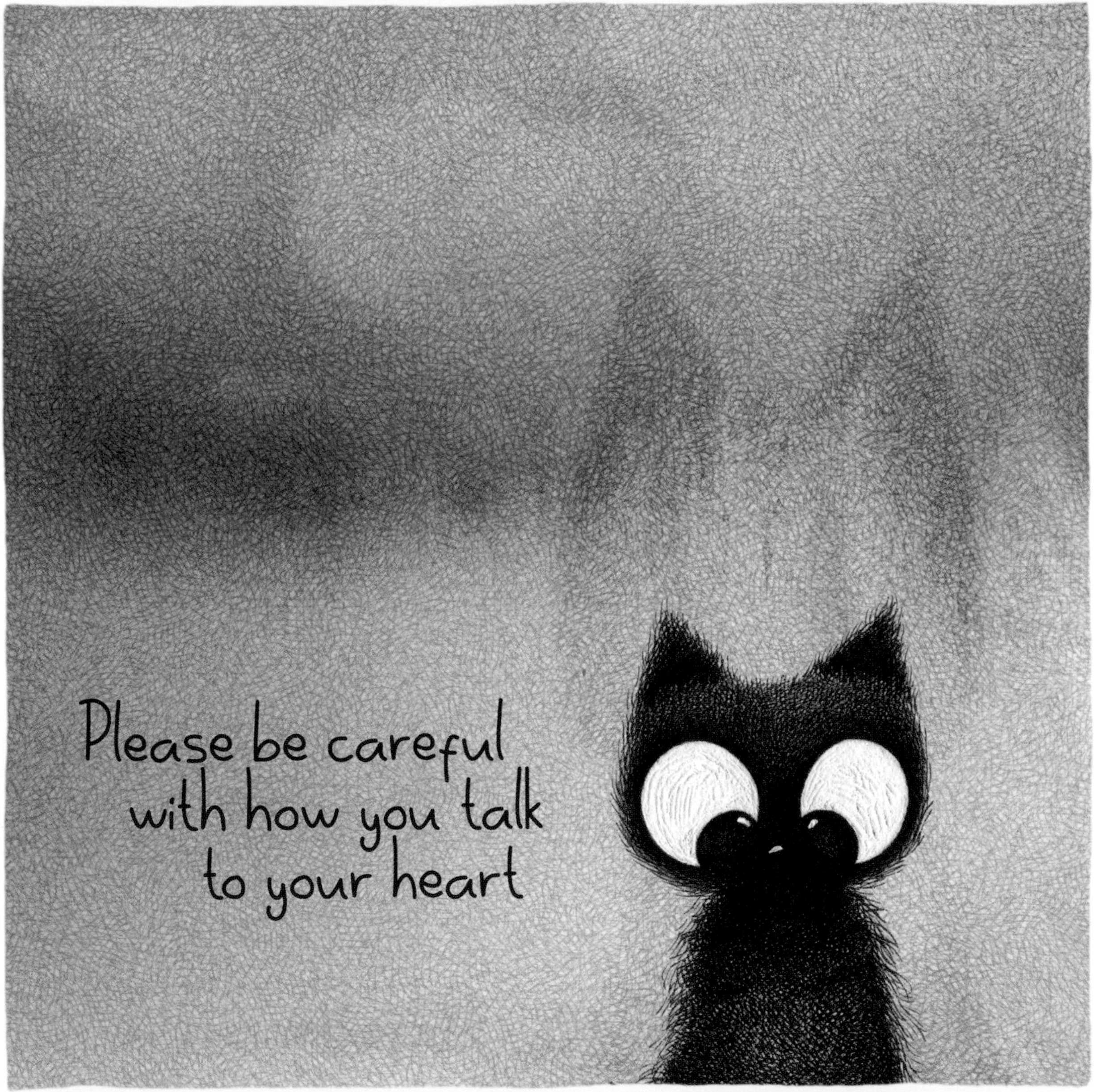
Please be careful
with how you talk
to your heart

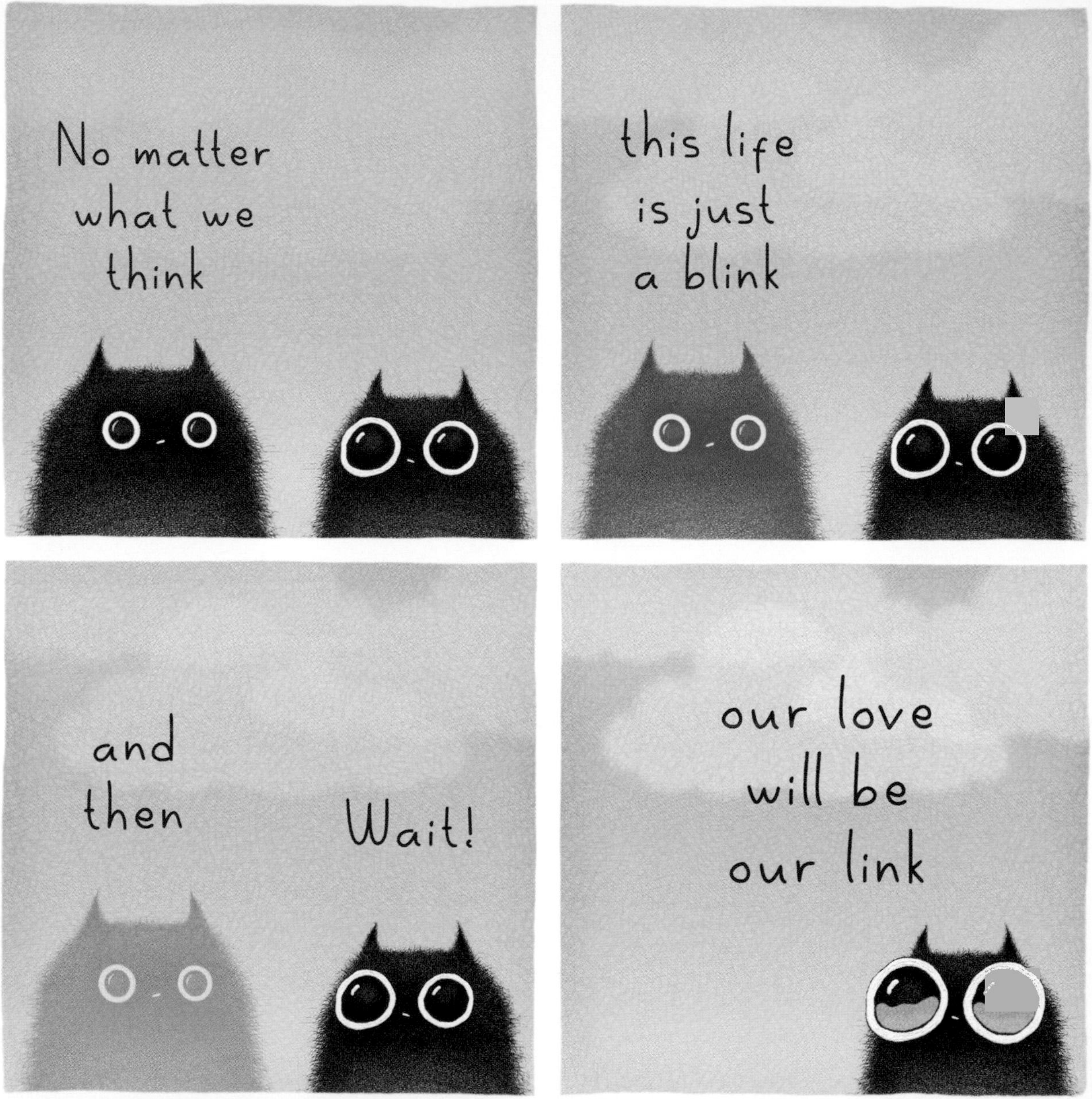
No matter
what we
think
this life
is just
a blink
and
then
Wait!
our love
will be
our link

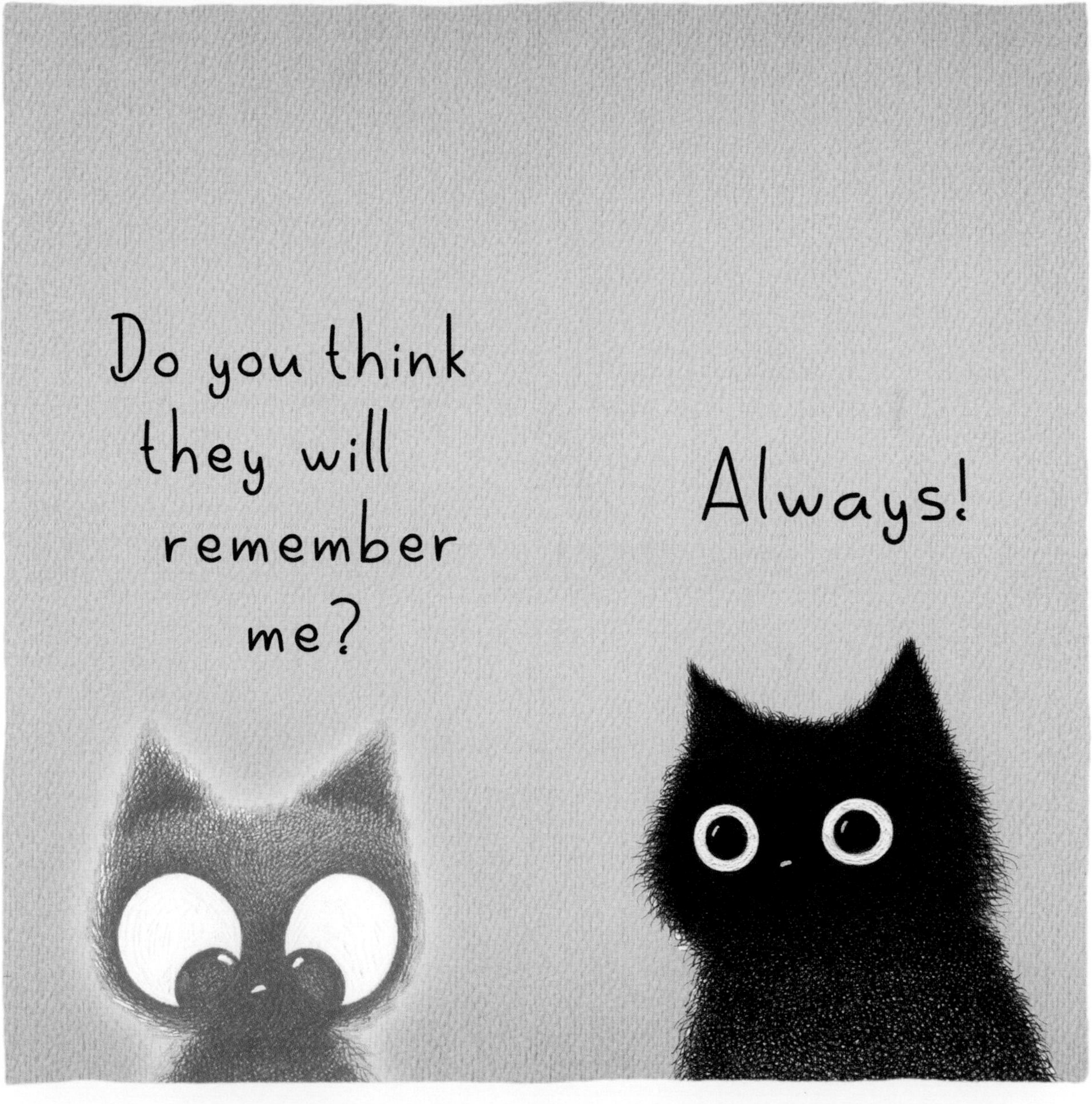
Do you think they will remember me?
Always!

My heartfelt thanks go to those who have walked with me on this book's creation journey, from brief encounters that ignited the spark of inspiration to constant support that transformed a vision into reality. I extend my gratitude to you as well, the reader, for choosing to embrace this work.

Andrews McMeel Publishing
a division of Andrews McMeel Universal
1130 Walnut Street, Kansas City, Missouri 64106

www.andrewsmcmeel.com

24 25 26 27 28 TEN 10 9 8 7 6 5 4 3 2 1

ISBN: 978-1-5248-9204-3

Library of Congress Control Number: 2024934334

Editor: Patty Rice
Art Director: Holly Swayne
Production Editor: Jennifer Straub
Production Manager: Chadd Keim

ATTENTION: SCHOOLS AND BUSINESSES
Andrews McMeel books are available at quantity discounts with bulk purchase for educational, business, or sales promotional use. For information, please e-mail the Andrews McMeel Publishing Special Sales Department: sales@amuniversal.com.

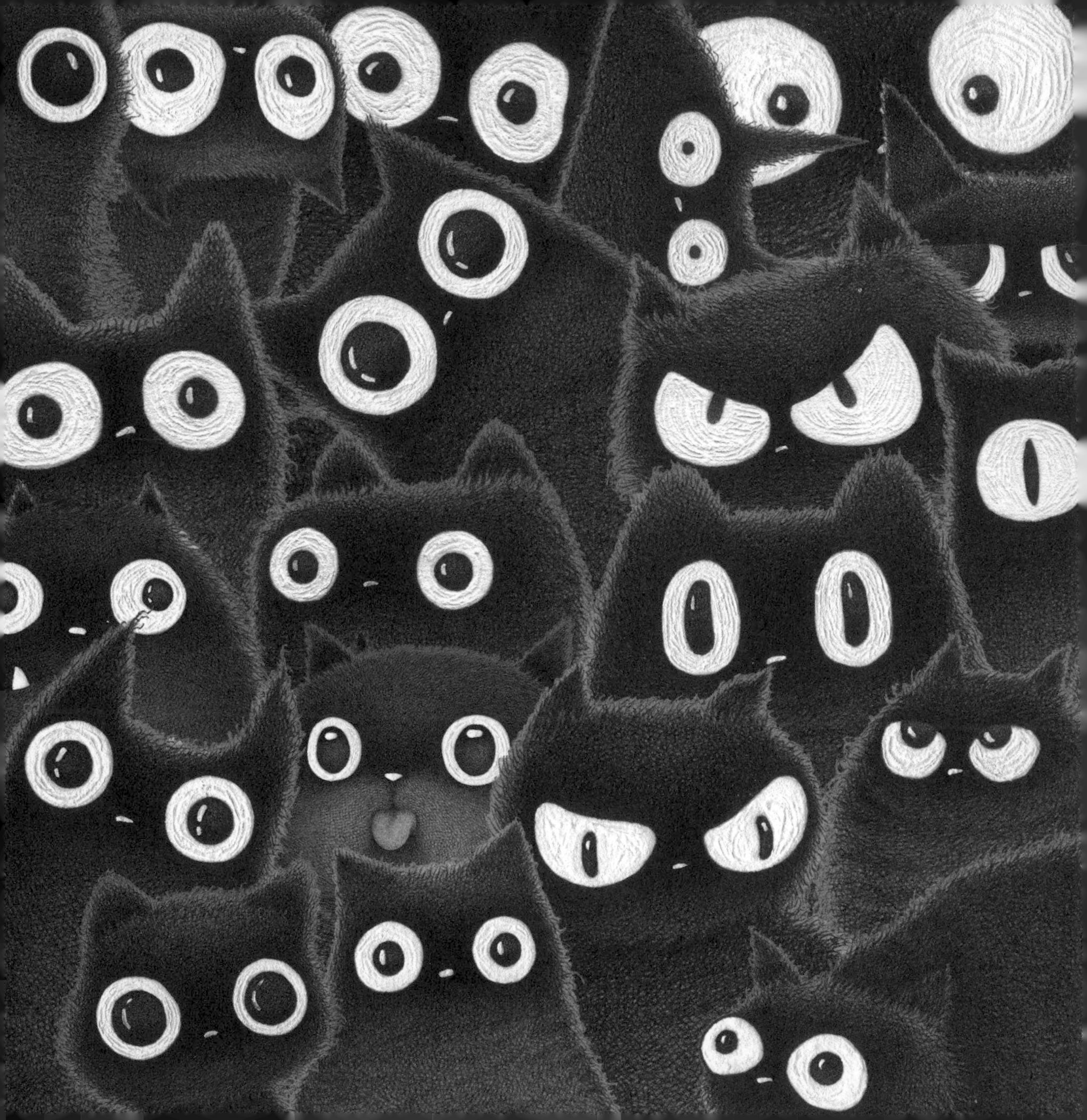